islam
— AND THE —
SON of GOD

D1399361

By the same author

Christ Above All:
Conversational Evangelism with People of Other Faiths

Islam: The House I Left Behind

For more information on Daniel Shayesteh's books

www.exodusfromdarkness.org

7spirits@gmail.com

islam
—AND THE—
SON of GOD

by **DANIEL SHAYESTEH**

Talesh Books

Scripture taken from the New King James Version.
Copyright © 1982 by Thomas Nelson, Inc. Used by
permission. All rights reserved.

Daniel Shayesteh, 1954–
Islam and the Son of God
Published by Talesh Books, Sydney, Australia.
ISBN: 978-0-9756017-3-0

A previous version of this book was
published as *The Difference is the Son*.

Talesh Books are distributed in the USA
and internationally by Ingram Book Group:
orders@ingrambook.com

Contents

Foreword

By Dr Michael York

We all know the tensions and often mistrust that exists between the East and the West in our world today. These divisions have deep historical roots and the scale of the differences often overwhelms us when we try and imagine a pathway to peace.

Islam and the Son of God is a significant book for all people who share a love of God's kingdom and God's blueprint for peace through Jesus Christ. This book represents the thoughts and feelings of a man who has seen and experienced the diverse cultural, religious and political landscapes of both the Middle-East and the West. As a result, the book provides a valuable perspective from one who is qualified to speak by the very nature of his personal journey.

In order to fully appreciate what Daniel has written here, it is helpful for the reader to know something about his journey.

Daniel was born in Northern Iran near the beautiful shores and hinterlands of the Caspian Sea. He grew up in a nominal Islamic farming family near a small city. His sharp intellect was identified early on and he was encouraged to be a servant of Islam. By the age of 9 he was able to recite the Qur'an in Arabic.

During his teenage years he became interested in Islamic aesthetic philosophy (*Erfaan*, similar to Sufism). During this time Daniel grew in his love of poetry and music.

He went off to a university in Tehran even though his family could only provide him with limited financial support. Daniel studied commerce and became a student communist during his first year of university. However, after reading various books on philosophy, he became convinced that there was one God for this universe. He therefore returned to Islam, but this time it was fundamentalist Islam.

Daniel was deeply involved in the Iranian Fundamentalist Revolution (1979) as a leading Muslim political leader and teacher of Islam in his homeland. Many years later he was saved wonderfully by Christ, when he escaped to Turkey after falling out of favor with Khomeini's political group.

Here is some of Daniel's story in his own words:

> "My wife, and I were born into nominal Muslim families in a city in the northern part of Iran. We became fully involved in the fundamentalist Islamic movement shortly after the 1979 Revolution. Our common interest in the movement drew us together and we were married. This involvement caused me to advance in the politically oriented religion Islam, and with the recognition and support of people in our city I announced my candidacy for the Islamic Parliament.
>
> The bitter rivalry of Islamic politics, which often leads to people being killed for their beliefs, meant I was a threat to Khomeini's political group who wanted to govern at any cost. I was kidnapped by Khomeini's Revolutionary Military and placed in a death cell to await a death sentence. God in his love and graciousness had other plans for my life and unexpectedly I was temporarily released. After two attempts, I escaped into Turkey where I was homeless and without family or friends. My loneliness was overwhelming at the time and I feared for my family's safety because of my escape. One year later in Turkey, through a business deal that went wrong, I came into contact with a Christian group who encouraged and supported me during this time.

One day I came to believe that the world and everything in it, including myself, was unjust. I started to complain to God saying "Aren't you the almighty God? Should I suffer all my life? What is this life for? How can I get out of this life?"

That night I heard the voice of Jesus in a dream, and the following Sunday I heard the preacher saying the exact words Jesus said to me in the dream: 'Come out of your father's old house and live in a new house on the rock of Jesus (based on Luke 6:48f). At the time, I didn't know that there is only one Almighty Name by which man can be saved.

Yes, only one Name -- Jesus.

The preacher's invitation created a desire in my heart to ask for a book which would give me knowledge of Jesus through His words. In this New Testament of the Bible I read, '. . . for just as through the disobedience of the one man the many were made sinners, so also through the obedience of the one man the many will be made righteous' (Romans 5:19). Logically and philosophically, I realized that all the fullness of the Deity lives in the second man (Jesus) (Colossians 2:9-10) and He is able to save sinners. This also, unlike the philosophy of other religions, revealed to me a new and genuine philosophy that God is personal and I can have an eternal relationship with Him.

Therefore, I believed in Him as my Creator, Savior and Deliverer.

Months later my wife and the children joined me in Turkey. My conversion came as a shock to my wife. 'How can a person change his or her religion and expose himself and his family to the danger of apostasy?' were her words, yet she recognized a change in me.

Some time later Jesus appeared to her in a dream, and through God's goodness and grace, my wife, who was once a fundamentalist Muslim, came to the Lord. Many months earlier God had given me a promise, 'Believe in the Lord Jesus and you will be saved, you and your household' (Acts 16:31). That day we worshipped together, 'Praise to you, Jesus. Be glorified in all the earth'."

On his arrival in Australia Daniel sought fellowship with Christians from Islamic backgrounds. In 1994 he commenced studies at Morling Bible College and completed the Diploma of Theology and Pastoral Ministry. He also has a Ph.D. in International Management, majoring in how culture and religion influences business and human attitudes.

Introduction

Throughout history many people have remained ignorant of important truths relating to life. Leaders, writers and orators have often been instrumental in reinforcing such ignorance. Religious leaders are not exempt from blame.

There have been innumerable examples of religious leaders taking advantage of ignorant listeners and in this way making extraordinary political, social and economic gains through their manipulative and/or untrue messages. Historical evidence highlights the gravity of the situation when an ignorant leader comes to power.

The task of awakening people to the reality that they have been deceived has not been an easy one. Many people have lost their lives in the process of trying to do this.

I am convinced that, despite bans on free press and threats against advocates of free speech in many countries, we still have a responsibility to stimulate people to search for the truths concerning life. Mankind has been created with the potential to discover truth and to live in peace and unity.

My life in both Islam and Christianity, with all its pains and joys, has brought me to the stage of wanting to communicate my concern for truth. Blind adherence to leadership and traditions results from ignorance and breeds disunity and animosity among individuals and nations of the world. The material of this book is not meant to cause religious competition that takes advantage of ignorance but rather to open eyes and expose ignorance. Nor is it meant to produce hatred between people of different religious persuasions, but rather to provide a space for thought, evaluation and decision. Hatred is an impediment to discovery.

From the outset I want to say that every human life, whether enemy or friend, is precious. Indeed, I want to encourage the loving of others regardless of their rank, race, religion, nationality or other distinction.

The point of view expressed by any sacred writing will certainly have an impact on society making it essential that the views are tested for the well-being of that society and mankind in general. In some countries, ignorance is encouraged, and people are not free to read their sacred writings. This prevents them from understanding and comparing their scriptures with other sacred works. Religious leaders are then free to interpret these sacred writings for their own political gain to legitimize lying, stealing, killing, terrorism and similar activities. Such authorities do not allow questioning. When such authority is coupled with ignorance, the result is religious practices being imposed that are sometimes at odds with the original beliefs of the culture. Millions of people live under such control today. To move from such oppression, ignorance must be replaced by freedom to search and discover truth. We need to assist people to distinguish between true and false beliefs so we can live together in peace with God and people.

Many people believe in war and enmity between people, but the human heart cries out for love and peace. A heart filled with peace radiates peace to those around. This is because the heart is the central tool in relationships with both God and humankind. If our hearts are in harmony with God, we will then become capable of loving others, resulting in peaceful relationships with God the Creator and one another. God's love allows us to engage in relationships based on mutual respect, trust and reciprocal obligation. However, war and enmity between people produces a society characterized by unease and instability.

The nations of the world are in desperate need of loving hearts and for this to happen, we need to engage in a wholehearted drive against the spirit of enmity, war, ignorance and neglect of humankind. This directive can only take place through openness, sincere investigation and acceptance. As the need of people for a peaceful relationship with God and each other are met, they will put aside bigotry, fanaticism, nationalism and war.

Writing this book has brought mixed emotions. I have experienced tears, fear, courage, laughter, anger, patience, disappointment and hope at different times. But in the end, it has resulted in a sincere and pervasive inner confidence that the people of the world can be disarmed of any reason for division from each other. The hope of Jesus, the Son of God, was always with me throughout these experiences, strengthening me as I reflected on His unconditional love in my heart.

The overriding goal of this book is to provide a practical comparison of the Qur'an and the Bible by analyzing the impact of the teachings of each on the lives of humanity in all of its dimensions. My earnest prayer is that readers may discover the source of unconditional love and welcome the true and peaceful God into their lives. Also, my hope is that they will become agents of peace bridging the walls of hostility between the peoples of the world.

1

The Genesis of Islam

Background

Foundations for a Prophetic Career

Islam—Beliefs and Practices

The New Faith Spreads

Muhammad's Political and Religious Thought

Background

Muhammad was the founder of Islam. He claimed to be the prophet of Allah, who revealed his words (the words of the *Qur'an* a.k.a. Koran) to Muhammad through the angel Gabriel. It is therefore instructive to consider Muhammad's background and the experiences that shaped his life in order to make a comparison with the life and standards of Jesus Christ, the Son of God.

Muhammad first lived in the city of Mecca and was strongly influenced by the Jewish and Christian religious values that were widely spread in the Arabian Peninsula and the neighboring countries.

From Islam's early traditions, we learn that during Muhammad's youth in Mecca he had contact with Christians and learned much from their faith. He also met enslaved scholars from different religious and cultural backgrounds[1] who played a significant role in building his relationship with the Christian churches in Mecca and Syria, and in building his theology.

However, it was at the age of forty when Muhammad called himself Allah's messenger. He said he had been sent to warn and guide the people of Arabia (c.f. Q[2].6:92; 41:44) and to call them to worship Allah[3]. He began preaching in Mecca around

---

1   Muhammad-bin Jarir Tabari, *Tarikh-al-rosol val-molouk (The History of Prophets and Kings),* Tehran: translated from Arabic into Persian by Abolghasem Payandeh, Asatir Pub., 1996 (1375 Hijra), PP.1299-1302. & Ibn Hisham, *Sirat Rasul Allah, (The Life of Muhammad,* translation by R. E. Ibn M. Hamadani), Tehran: Ershad Islami Pub., 1998 (1377 Hijra), PP.189-192. . & N. Anderson, *The World's Religions,* England: Inter Varsity Press, 1994, P.93. & G. Nehls, *Christians Ask Muslims,* Nairobi: Life Challenge Pub., 1992, P.47.

2   "Q" stands for Qur'an.

3   Allah is the generic term for God in many middle-eastern cultures. Allah is identified as one of the 360 or so idols worshipped by the Arabian people for centuries before Muhammad was born. Many

610 A.D. and did so for about twelve years before migrating to Medina. Those who believed in the oneness of Allah and accepted Muhammad as his messenger were called Muslims. "Muslim" is an Arabic word that means "one who submits" (to Allah) (c.f.Q.29:46c). "Islam" is Arabic for submission.

Foundations for a Prophetic Career

The Influence of the Poetic and Angelic Culture

Poetry is one of the oldest, most attractive and honorable ways of communication in all civilizations. Poets in every nation have won the respect of many people from generation to generation. Even hundreds of years after the death of some poets, the study of their poetry is kept alive through their followers. Some of them are promoted to the level of prophethood by their followers because of their broad spiritual journey and discovery. Many people in the Middle East aspire to be poets, and in this way win the respect of their people. There is a common belief among people that a poet will never die in the mind and heart of the people. The poet's timeless words about life will always find eternal expression through the tongues of future generations.

In Arabia, poetry was rooted in the mind and heart of the people and played a significant role in individual and tribal relationships long before the rise of Muhammad. The most successful poets gained the favor of people socially, politically, economically and religiously. It was a great joy to an Arab tribe when a poet appeared in one of its families. Celebrations were held for such an honorable moment, and people from other

---

do not know that Allah was the moon god of the Arabians. This explains the crescent moon found on the minarets of mosques and the flags of Muslim nations. Islamic books reveal that "Allah" was the name of a pagan God in Saudi Arabia (Bukhari :: Volume 3 :: Book 49 :: Hadith 862 & Muslim :: Book 19 : Hadith 4401 & Dawud :: Book 19 : Hadith 2998). Historical writings also identify Allah with Baal.

tribes joined the celebrations and congratulated the family and the tribe. Poetry was so important that whenever the families met each other, they wished each other the birth of a poet boy.[1] The life of a tribe was very much dependent upon warrior poets whose tongues were even sharper than their swords in order to raise and strengthen the bravery of their members and to weaken their enemies. One reason that Ayatollah Khomeini was successful in preparing many younger Iranians for martyrdom in the war between Iran and Iraq was his success in getting some younger poets to vocalize or sing war poems in a nomadic Arabic style for retaliation. The mourning songs, which were in memory of martyrs, were implemented in a way in order to bring glory to martyrs and also prepare people to join the war and make it victorious.

In Muhammad's time, poets devoted themselves to guiding, defending and caring for the members of their tribe and to gaining glory for the tribe. All aspects of these responsibilities were portrayed in the structure of the poems (*ghasida*, or *qasida*, and *rajaz*) and were recited wherever the situation made it appropriate.

In times of war, poems were recited in order to recall the glories of past warriors and to weaken the spirit of the enemies by ridiculing, reviling and holding them up to shame.[2] The purpose of the Arab warriors was not only to win the war, but also to gain glory for their tribe. The joy and glory of this victory led people to express the glorification of the tribe in poems and to pass them from generation to generation as a mark of honor to that tribe. This poetic language was common throughout Arabia. Mecca, as the center of pagan shrines and religious poetry, played a significant role in spreading the poems through its many pilgrims.

---

1 Read R. A. Nicholson, *Literary History of the Arabs,* England: Curzon Press Ltd, 1993 (first published in 1907), P.71.

2 D. M. Lang (Editor), *Guide to Eastern Literature,* Great Britain: C. Tinling & Co. Ltd., 1971, P.3. & R. A. Nicholson, P.74.

Muhammad was a clever Arab boy gifted in poetry and furthermore privileged by the many opportunities he received since his grandfather became his guardian. After many years of travel and experience with his uncle between Mecca and Syria, he gained the courage to authorize the usage of commonly practiced and influential poetry as part of his ministry; a ministry of renouncing the lesser gods and praising Allah as the superior one of all. He grew up in Mecca and shared the excitement of the powerful poetic culture with his influential tribe, which was the custodian of the holy shrine, *Ka'ba*. A century before Muhammad, his tribe *Quraish*, rose to power in Mecca, multiplied its influence and thereby prospered socially, politically, economically and religiously. The Ka'ba attracted large crowds of pagan pilgrims from all over the Peninsula. This not only increased the religious power of the Quraish, but also prospered them materially.[1] Muhammad, therefore, proudly carried the honor of his influential tribe and practiced its religious customs wherever he went. Like his forefathers, he was interested in promoting religious acts in any way he could, whether it was idol worshipping, meditation at the Mount of Hira (a shrine for pagans) or the commonly accepted poetic recitation. The Qur'an also confirms that up to the point of Allah's calling of Muhammad at the age of forty, he was considered "lost" as a result of practicing the religion of his tribe (Q.93:7).

Poetic culture was very strong among the members of Muhammad's immediate and extended family. Prior to Muhammad's prophetic claim, his first wife Khadijah wrote very encouraging poems saying that she would enthusiastically wait for her beloved husband to announce himself as a prophet.[2] Muhammad's uncle, Abutalib, was also a poet. He wrote numerous poems about his nephew, Muhammad, and sent them out to the public. He did this in order to gain the

---

1   Read R. A. Nicholson, PP.64-65.

2   Ibn Hisham, *Sirat Rasul Allah,* PP.169-72.

kindness of the people towards Muhammad, using this as a shield to protect his nephew against his opponents who wanted to hurt him because of his opposition to pagan worship. Poems were used in every aspect of life and it should be noted that Muhammad and his followers never abandoned Arabian poetic culture after the rise of Islam. Islamic traditions record many poems that were written for various occasions in order to strengthen the Islamic movement and also to weaken their enemies and opponents.

Arabian poets believed that no one could become an authentic poet unless a *jinni*[1], or spirit, appeared to him, possessed his soul and forced him to recite the inspired words of his mouth. Anyone who experienced the inspiring words of the spirits in such a way was highly respected by these people. Muhammad spoke in a similar way about his revelation, saying that a spirit revealed the revelation to him and forced him to recite the inspired verses from his mouth. From the earliest beginnings of his ministry, he always wanted to include the religious values of his nation along with the beliefs of surrounding people. Not only did he say that the Jewish and Christian priests predicted his prophet-hood, but that the pagan priests also knew that he would be a prophet in the future. He asserted that every night Satan ascended to heaven, heard the latest news from the spirits and came back to the pagan priests in Mecca and in this way spread the news among the people prior to Muhammad's claim.[2] For this reason, he named the chapter 72 of the Qur'an after jinnis for the great role they played in spreading the new of his prophet-hood and spoke in favor of them:

---

1 People believed that there were good and bad jinnis (jinns or spirits) both created by Allah from fire. They are powerful and intelligent creatures who serve the cause of Allah (cf. Q.15:27). Muhammad believed that some jinns accepted Islam (Muslim :: Book 26 : Hadith 5559). Satan is the head of jinns in Islam.

2 Ibn Hisham, *Sirat Rasul Allah*, PP.178-9.

> *It has been revealed to me that a company of Jinns listened (to the Qur'an). They said, 'We have really heard a wonderful Recital'* (Q.72:1).

Although Muhammad withdrew himself from his former religious practices, he kept his highly influential poetic and angelic beliefs, persuading people to believe in his recitations. These recitations are the verses of the Qur'an.

Curiously, Muhammad did not call himself a poet (cf. Q.69:38-43) and even denigrated poets (Q.26:224-226) in his second Meccan ministry. Even though he did not consider himself a poet, the people regarded him as one because of the poetic style he used:

> *And* (people) *said, 'Shall we then abandon our god* (idols) *for a crazed poet?'* (Q.37:36)

Muhammad's attitude is astonishing as half of the Qur'an was recited in an Arabic poetic style.[1]

At the first revelation (calling) the spirit (jinni) caught Muhammad forcefully and squeezed him so hard until his neck muscles twitched with terror. Muhammad felt as though he was being suffocated. He could no longer bear the pressure of the angel and therefore let the angel take control over him and make him repeat his words.[2] Muhammad claimed himself to be a prophet due to such an "inescapable" experience in order to convince people that his ministry was from above - authentic and irreversible.

---

1 R. Tames, *The Muslim World,* London: Macdonald & Co., Ltd., Pub., 1982, P.16. & R. A. Nicholson, P.159.

2 Ibn Hisham, *Sirat Rasul Allah,* P.209. & Read the narratives in Phil Parshall, *Inside the Community,* USA: Baker Books, 1994, PP.18-21. & K. Armstrong, *A History of God,* London: Heinemann Pub., 1993, P.161-3.

The Influence of the Followers of the "One God"

Muhammad's journeys, as a caravan trader[1], took him far from his hometown, Mecca, increasing his knowledge about the beliefs and lifestyles of other nations. This new understanding coupled with the strong relationships he had with knowledgeable religious people at home and abroad guided his revolutionary decision to reject idolatry and to worship one God (c.f. Q.16:103; 6:105).

In Muhammad's time, two superpowers, the Byzantine (Roman) and the Sasanid (Persian) Empires had dominated different parts of the Arabian Peninsula, but Arabia was not a conquered nation[2]. Syria was in the hands of the Byzantine Empire, while the Persian Empire ruled areas such as Iraq and Yemen. The Roman and Persian empires experienced six centuries of constant military, political and commercial rivalry that resulted in their domination of the above lands. However, the impassability of the Arabian Desert caused both empires to limit the operation of their armies to the central settlements of the area.[3] The only leverage that the West could rely upon in order to win the allegiance of the area was the evangelistic aspect of its religion, Christianity (unlike Zoroastrianism, the dominant religion of the East that did not believe in religious evangelism for reaching out to people). Therefore, Christianity played a significant role in the lives of the Roman-ruled people. Christian missionaries were encouraged to reach out to the non-Christian communities wherever they could.

1　Muhammad was a caravan trader, first working for his uncle and then for his first and future wife, Khadijah.

2　B. W. Sherratt and D. J. Hawkin, *Gods and Men,* London: Blackie and Son Ltd, 1972, P. 74. & G. Wiet, V. Elisseeff, P. Wolff and J. Naudou, *The Great Medieval Civilisations*(Vol. III), London: George Allen and Unwin Ltd., 1975, P. 144. & Armstrong, PP.158-9. & V. Bailey and Wise, E., *Muhammad: his times and influence*, Edinburgh: W & R Chambers Ltd, 1976, P.8.

3　J. B. Glubb, *A Short History of the Arab People*, London: Quartet Books, PP.21, 1969, 23.

The Syrian Christians were also religiously and politically in favor of and in harmony with the Byzantine Empire. Therefore, the contemporary Church of Syria in Muhammad's time was trying hard to ensure that their contemporary Christian missions could flourish in Mecca and the surrounding areas. They realized that the Arabian businessmen were more interested in the Western way of life than in the Eastern way of life. Syrian Christians eagerly used this attraction to the Western way of life in their approach to Arabs. This also helped them to combat the activities of the Nestorian Christians of Iraq who were in favor of the Eastern way of life and who had been trying to spread their Babylonian culture to their neighbors, including the Arabian Peninsula.[1]

There were two ways the expansion of Christianity could benefit those Catholic Christians living under Persian rule; those living in Iraq[2] in the northern part of the Arabian Desert, in Yemen, and in Nejran in the southern parts of the Arabian Desert. First, the influence of Christians in this area could be strengthened thus aligning themselves more with the Byzantine Empire, which in turn might expand this empire's dominion, freeing them from the Persian Empire's present and future threats and persecutions. Second, they could easily identify themselves with the West as the center of the Christian Empire, the source of Christian missionary effort and many other provisions as well.

From the time of his youth, Muhammad made various trips to *Sham* (Syria) accompanying his uncle, Abutalib, serving as a helper with his caravan. His close relationship with his uncle and Christians created a leaning in him toward the Catholic Church. Because of this interest, he gained favor with Bahira (or Buhaira), a priest from Sham, and with Nofel (or Naufal),

---

1 R. A. Nicholson, P.138.

2 The majority of Christians in Iraq were of the Nestorian sect, which was called heretical by the Byzantine Church (J. B. Glubb, P.26).

a priest from Mecca. Nofel was a Hanifite[1] from Muhammad's own tribe, Quraish, who had converted into Christianity many years before the rise of Muhammad as prophet. Nofel was a notable Christian leader in Mecca, who was very old at the time of Muhammad's youth. Nofel arranged for Muhammad to work for his niece Khadijah, who was a widowed merchant.[2] Muhammad eventually married Khadijah. Through this marriage, he became more involved in religious matters relating to the one God. Islamic tradition says that Bahira, Nofel and Khadijah all knew that Muhammad would become a prophet and encouraged him to undertake the task.[3] After Muhammad received his first revelation, Nofel continually contacted him, confirming to him the revelation he had received and encouraging him to announce the prophecy.[4] But, interestingly, Nofel's name is not among the names of those who became Muslim.[5]

Muhammad, therefore, was strongly affected by the contemporary Jewish and Christian belief of monotheism and this was one of the factors that influenced him to oppose the idolatry of Mecca.[6] The teachers and the knowledgeable people who surrounded Muhammad also had a profound effect in shaping the future doctrine of Islam. Muhammad's own contemporaries blamed him of borrowing words from an enslaved Christian called "Jabr".[7] Another one of the enslaved scholars who met with Muhammad was an ex-Zoroastrian (and ex-Catholic after accepting Islam), Salman Farsi. Salman's part

---

1   Refer to the footnote 1 in page 20 for the word 'Hanif'.

2   Ibn Hisham, *Sirat Rasul Allah,* P.168.

3   Ibid., PP.158-61,168.

4   Ibid., P.107.

5   Ibid., PP.210,214-32.

6   Y. Armajani, *Middle East Past and Present,* Prentice-Hall, 1970, PP.30-31. & Riadh El Droubie, *Islam,* London: Ward Lock Educational Co., Ltd, 1983, P.7.

7   Ibn Hisham, P.180.

in laying the foundation for Muhammad's activities was highly significant.

Salman's life was an interesting one. He was a Zoroastrian from infancy and a magus highly experienced in the rituals and the beliefs of Zoroastrianism. However, while in his country, Iran, he went to a church in the city of Esfahan and became disinterested in Zoroastrianism. In turn he became more interested in Christianity.[1] Eventually, he travelled to Syrian and joined a Catholic church and got involved in Christian ministry. Throughout his Christian ministry, he visited some churches in Iraq, a Persian state. Afterward, he returned to Syria and at the advice of a prominent Christian leader he organized a journey to Arabia with the hope of seeing Muhammad in a Catholic Church in Mecca. On the way, he was assaulted and sold by the caravan drivers as a slave. This led him to Medina, ruining his hopes of seeing Muhammad in Mecca. However, years after when Muhammad immigrated to Medina, he released Salman who became a significant figure in the Islamic movement.[2]

Salman's various religious experiences created significant insight into Muhammad's mind when they spent time together. A comparison made in the following table proves how much Salman's knowledge and revolutionary background shaped Muhammad's religious-political life. The comparison between the historical foundations of Zoroastrianism and Islam brings forth the idea that, in all likelihood, Muhammad's revolutionary

---

1 We understand from Zoroastrian history that the Magi, who came to visit the baby Christ, were sent by the king of ancient Iran, Hormoz. The journey and the visit were given a valuable place in the religious memories and were considered as blessings to the land and people of Iran (The Yasna, book2 in Persian by Pourdavood, PP.167-172). This historical linkage between Christianity and Zoroastriansm might have been one of the reasons that Salman took refuge in Christianity.

2 Ibn Hisham, *Sirat Rasul Allah,* PP.95-98. & Muhammad-bin Jarir Tabari, *Tarikh-al-rosol val-molouk,* P.1301.

religious life was modeled on that of Zoroaster, the founder and the prophet of Zoroastrianism;[1]

Muhammad 570-623 A.D.	Zoroaster 569-492 B.C.?
He grew up at a time when his fellow Meccans worshiped many gods.	He grew up at a time when his fellow Persians worshiped many gods.
He was in relationship with some of the most knowledgeable individuals who lived at that time.	He was in relationship with some of the most knowledgeable individuals.
As he grew up, he spent much time meditating alone in mountain caves.	As he grew up, he spent much time meditating alone in mountain caves.

1 The following sources were used for the comparison between Islam and Zoroastrianism: Avesta: (Yasna, Gatha, Yashts, Visperd, Khordeh Avesta), research and translation into Persian by Hashem Razi, Forouhar Pub., 1995 (1374 Hijra), PP.19-20,26-28,33,230,370. & M. Rawlings, *Life-Wish: Reincarnation: Reality or Hoax,* Nashville: Thomas Nelson Inc., 1981. & M. Mueller, ed., *Secret Books of the East,* Oxford: Krishna Press, 1897-1910. & R. Cavendish, *The Great Religions,* London: Contact Pub., 1980, P.126. & J. A. Williams, *Islam,* Washington: Square Press, 1963, P.48. & J. R. Hinnells, *Dictionary of Religions,* Great Britain: Penguin Books, 1984, PP.361-2. & Hinnells, J. R., *Zoroastrianism and the Parsis,* Great Britain: Ward Lock Educational, 1981, PP..9,17,39,40,46,73. & J. B. Taylor, *Thinking about ISLAM,* Great Britain: Lutterworth Educational, 1971, P.27. & E. G. Parrinder, *A Book of World Religions,* Great Britain: Hulton Educational Pub., 1974, P.65. & The International Standard Bible Encyclopedia for Zoroastrianism. & R. Tames, P.27. & R. Zacharias, *Jesus Among Other Gods,* USA: Word Pub., 2000, P.190 (Footnote 3).

Muhammad 570-623 A.D.	Zoroaster 569-492 B.C.?
At the age of 40, he received a vision and then a second one that removed any doubt in him as being a prophet to win his countrymen away from the worship of many deities and win them to the service of one God.	At the age of 30, he received a vision and then other visions that removed any doubt in him as being a prophet to win his countrymen away from the worship of many deities and win them to the service of one God.
His first convert was his cousin (simultaneously with his wife).	His first convert was his cousin.
He had little success during his early ministry. The beginning of his success was when he traveled to Medina.	He had little success during his early ministry. The beginning of his success was when he traveled to Bactria.
His message at first was rejected and he was mocked and was forced to leave his hometown.	His message at first was rejected and he was mocked and was forced to leave his home.
He legitimized "holy war" (*jihad*) against idol worshipers and non-Muslims._	He legitimized "holy war"[1] against idol worshipers. Later, his followers waged "holy war" against Christians mainly because it was the enemy's (Rome's) official religion.
Muslims, with his guidance, quickly destroyed the widespread idol worship and established their own belief in one God, a heaven and a hell.	Zoroastrians under his guidance quickly destroyed the widespread idol worship and established their own belief in one God, a heaven and a hell.

Muhammad 570-623 A.D.	Zoroaster 569-492 B.C.?
By his followers, He is called superior and incomparable to all humankind, in the perfection of his holiness.	By his followers, He is called superior and incomparable to all humankind, in the perfection of his holiness.
At one point in his prophetic ministry, Muhammad had a journey to heaven (cf. Q.17:1).[2]	At one point in his prophetic ministry, Zoroaster had a journey to heaven.
Muslim prayers are said five times each day.	Zoroastrian prayers are said five times each day.[3]
Before praying, Muslims always wash ceremonially.	Before praying, the Zoroastrian always washes ceremonially.
Prayers are recited in the language of the Qur'an.	Prayers are recited in the language of Avesta.
A corpse is washed and wrapped ceremonially prior to burial.	A corpse is washed and wrapped ceremonially prior to burial.
Both Zoroastrianism and Islam are influenced by the pagan beliefs before them and by Judaism which was widely spread in Persia and Saudi Arabia. Also, these two religions similarly believe that after death both righteous and unrighteous will enter hell. It is from hell that those whose good deeds outweigh their bad will pass over a narrow bridge, as thin as a single hair, and enter heaven. The unrighteous, though, will remain in hell.	

So, Muhammad's 'One God' idea was one of the great factors that caused him to take up the prophetic ministry. This idea attracted those Arabs who valued the worship of the One God like their ancestor Ishmael. It is obvious from the Qur'an that many Arab nationals believed in One God (Q.23:84-90; 31:25-

26)[1]. In addition, we know from tradition that Muhammad's grandfather, Abdulmutallib, prayed to the *unique God* to protect Mecca from the invasion of Abraha, the governor of Yeman. Also, at the birth of Muhammad, he took the baby to the sanctuary and praised the *Almighty God* for his newborn grandchild.[2] Therefore, monotheism, the belief in One God, was not a revolutionary idea to the Meccan community. However, taking a stand against the idolatry rampant in Mecca was revolutionary.

The early ministry of Muhammad, as the early writers of Islam[3] have pointed out, was not totally associated with the proclamation of the 'One God' idea. There were times in Muhammad's prophetic ministry when he exalted the three idols[4], *al-Lot* (goddess of fertility), *al-Uzza* (goddess of power) and *Manat* (goddess of fate) (mentioned in the Qur'an 53:19-

---

1   'Hanif' was a religious group in the Arabian Peninsula, who proclaimed belief in one God, the God of Abraham, and rejected the polytheistic worship before the rise of Muhammad. They were neither Jews nor Christians but Arabs who were from Muhammad's own tribe, Quraish (R. Machatschke, P.3. & K. Armstrong, P.160: narrates from Muhammad's first biographer Ibn Ishaq). Muhammad called Hanifies the people of Abraham, and Abraham a Hanifite [Q.3:95; 4:125; 6:161].

2   Ibn Hisham, *Sirat Rasul Allah*, PP.74-79,144. & Muhammad-bin Jarir Tabari, *Tarikh-al-rosol val-molouk*, P.708.

3   Muhammad-bin Jarir Tabari, *Commentary on the Qur'an* (translated from Arabic into Persian 972-987 AD), Tehran: Tehran University Pub., 1977 (1356 Hijra), PP.1769-71. & Muhammad-bin Jarir Tabari, *Tarikh-al-rosol val-molouk*, P.881.

4   Al-Lot was worshipped by the tribe of Saghif who were from Taef. Al-Uzza was worshipped by the tribes of Quraish, Bani-Kananeh and Bani-Salim. Manat was worshipped by the tribes of Auss, Khazraj and Ghassan (A. M. A. Shahrestani, *Tozih-almelal (Almelal Valnahl)*, Iran: Translated by S. M. Jalali-Naieni, Eghbal Pub., 1982 (1361 Hijra), P.386 of book2.

20[1]) by saying that they were divine beings assisting Allah in his work. The exaltation of these idols was not in accordance with the philosophy of Muhammad's 'One God' ministry.

Major setbacks for Muhammad (in his late forty's) were the loss of his encouraging and loyal wife, Khadijah, and the loss of his uncle, Abutalib, who was like a shield for his nephew.[2] Along with this he did not have any influential political friends, who could shield him from the political pressures that abounded at that time. As a result, he felt lonely and became more vulnerable to his pain and the pressures brought on by the unfriendly atmosphere created by the Meccan leaders against him and his friends. Because of this pressure he decided to make a slight change to his political stance in order to gain the favor of his opponents. To this end, he spoke in favor of their idols and this, in turn, gained him the ability to survive in Mecca for some years.

Nevertheless, this political stance in favor of idols was not to last. In his later revelations in Medina, when Islam was gaining more power, Muhammad mentioned that there are some verses in the Qur'an that were instigated by Satan with the permission of Allah. He said that Allah was aware of them and allowed them to be included in the pages of the Qur'an initially, but now desired them to be removed from the pages of the Qur'an by his prophet;

---

1 These verses are known as *Satanic Verses.* After verse 19 in Q.53, the verse that exalted the three idols mentioned in verse 19 was, "These are the exalted females, and truly their intercession may be expected". Later it was replaced by the text as it now stands *(cf.* Q.22:51-52).

2 P. W. Crittenden, *Islam,* London: Macmillan Education Ltd, 1972, P.7. & Muhammad-bin Jarir Tabari, *Commentary on the Qur'an* (translated from Arabic into Persian 972-987 AD for the fist time), Tehran: Tehran University Pub., 1977 (1356 Hijra), P.1689.

Those who strive to invalidate our signs shall be inmates of Hell. We have not sent any apostle or prophet before thee, among whose desires Satan injected not some wrong desires, but God shall bring to nought that which Satan had suggested. Thus God shall affirm His revelations for God is Knowing, Wise! That He may make that which Satan hath injected, a trial to those in whose hearts is a disease, and whose hearts are hardened. – Verily, the wicked are in a far-gone severance from the truth! (Q.22:51-53).

Some people criticized Muhammad for the replacement of the already revealed verses of the Qur'an with the new ones. As is obvious from verse 51, he calls his critics unbelieving people who are destined for hell. In verse 53, he calls them those 'whose hearts are hardened' and therefore, they cannot accept that Muhammad can change the verses of the Qur'an. However, Ibn Hisham (the writer of Muhammad's biography) also asserts that those verses of exaltation that Muhammad said in favor of the idols were the words of his mouth but they were instigated by *Satan*.[1]

As mentioned earlier, historical evidence shows that the word "Allah" was the name of the great idol in Mecca, to which the forefathers of Muhammad offered their praise and honor.[2] The choosing of the phrase *"Allah, the best creator of all"* in Q.23:14 might indicate that Muhammad's inner desire was to encourage his people to join him. By using a name they knew, and using it for the real God, he made a bridge for his people to cross from their old beliefs to belief in the "best creator of all," Allah. This, he possibly thought, could attract contemporary Arabs to have an interest in his call.

---

1 Ibn Hisham, *Sirat Rasul Allh*.PP.165-167. & A. Guillaume: '*Islam*', London: Penguin Books, 1954, P.189.

2 R. Machatschke, *Islam: The Basics,* London: SCM Press Ltd, 1995, P.10.

The Effect of a Tolerant and Influential Tribe

A third factor that influenced Muhammad to undertake the prophetic ministry was his tribe. He was a member of Hashimi's clan, a dominant and influential tribe in Mecca called Quraish[1] that was the custodian of the sacred shrine of Ka'bah. (SAME AS KA'BA). The Hashimi's leadership in particular, and the Quraishi's in general, seemed much more tolerant toward those who converted into the One-God faith. This tolerance was because of their settlement in urban areas, having abandoned their nomadic way of life and being involved in trading with other parts of the world. Their relationship with other nations produced some cultural changes and flexibility compared to their primary Bedouin culture. As a result, some could dare to choose their preferred way of life, rather than hold rigidly to their old culture.

Prior to Muhammad's acceptance as a prophet, there were people from the tribe of Quraish, some even from Muhammad's own relatives and friends, who took advantage of the tribe's tolerant leadership. They left the paganism of Quraish and joined the One-God worshipping group of Hanafi. One of them was the aforementioned Nofel, influential in the Christian church in Mecca.[2] Membership of such an influential and tolerant tribe provided Muhammad with a safe haven.[3] This enabled him

---

1 Y. Armajani, PP.27-29.

2 In addition, there was Ubaydollah ibn Jahsh, Muhammad's cousin, Othman ibn Alhovaireth, who went to Rome and became a Christian, and Zeyd ibn Amr, who was the uncle of Umar ibn al-Khattab, one of Muhammad's father-in-laws, his closest companion and the second Caliph of the Islamic empire. It is said that Zeyd hoped to be sent as a prophet to the Arabs, and he opposed Muhammad's prophetic claim (Ibn Hisham, *Sirat Rasul Allah,*PP.198-202. & A. M. A. Shahrestani, *Tozih-almelal,* P.399 of book2. & K. Armstrong, P.160. & R. A. Nicholson (states Ibn Ishaq's comment), P.149-150).

3 Muhammad-bin Jarir Tabari, *Tarikh-al-rosol val-molouk,* P.872. & Ibn Hisham, *Sirat Rasul Allah,*PP.414,418.

to gain momentum so he could eventually follow a direction similar to his converted relatives and friends. Muhammad announced himself as a prophet sent to the Arabs and he soon gathered around him Arabs and slaves who were seeking to escape their paganism and slavery.

However, although the tribe was influential, there came a time when this influence declined due to the death of those who provided significant support for Muhammad. As a result, Muhammad had no choice but to immigrate from Mecca to Medina.

The Effect of a Scheming Wife

Her wealth and links with Medina

The fourth factor that influenced Muhammad to undertake the prophetic ministry was his marriage to Khadijah. Khadijah had strong trading links with cities like Medina and Syria, and this marriage gained him great wealth and many Christian relatives and friends and provided him with a status consistent with that of a prophet. This great wealth financed his initial step to be a prophet and his new relatives strongly encouraged him, giving him confidence to continue his ministry.[1]

Her Poems

Muhammad's ministry was initially tough going. In the first three years after the first revelation, he felt as though he had been forgotten by Allah and even admitted having suicidal thoughts in his mind.[2] However, his faithful and insisting wife never left him alone and stood firmly beside him helping him to overcome his disappointments so that he could fulfill his prophetic ministry. Her poems to him were most encouraging,

---

1 For further information read, Muhammad-bin Jarir Tabari, *Tarikh-al-rosol val-molouk*, PP.850-1. & Ibn Hisham, *Sirat Rasul Allah,*PP.158-61,168. & N. Anderson, P.94.

2 Read N.L. Geisler & Abdul Saleeh, *Answering Islam,* USA: Baker Books, 1997, PP.71,156. & B. W. Sherratt, P.78.

prompting him to take the prophetic ministry as seriously as possible and he made himself available for more religious preaching and activities.

Her Persuasion

We learn from Islam's early reliable sources[1] that Muhammad himself was not able to distinguish the source of the voice that he first heard calling for him to be a prophet. He thought it possible that an evil spirit had possessed him. To be possessed by an evil spirit (Satan) was not strange or a thing to be detested according to Muhammad's cultural background. However, it was a serious issue for his wife Khadijah. According to the ancient Arabs, the best men of the tribes were those who were in league with and dependent upon evil spirits and achieved an extraordinary role in bringing glory to the tribe.[2] This helps us to understand that Muhammad was not so much worried about being possessed by Satan, but was more concerned by his wife's reaction to the event. This assertion is supported by Muhammad's latter Meccan ministry, when he affirmed the belief of his forefathers calling the spirits (jinns or djinns) the servants of whom both Allah and his prophets were pleased with (cf.Q.34:12-13). When Muhammad shared with his wife that an evil spirit had possessed him, her immediate reaction was 'this cannot be, I have hope that you will be the prophet of these people'. She went to her uncle Nofel, the priest of the nearby church in Mecca, and recounted the story to him in order to obtain a view in line with her own. Having a political agenda, the priest believed it wise to share this view. As Khadija and Nofel were the two most powerful influences in his life, Muhammad was soon persuaded to claim himself as a prophet in Mecca. Nofel, the leader of the church in Mecca, was

---

1 Ibn Hisham, *Sirat Rasul Allah*,PP.212-3. & Muhammad-bin Jarir Tabari, *Tarikh-al-rosol val-molouk*, P.851. & Muhammad-bin Jarir Tabari, *Tarikh-al-rosol val-molouk*, P.2034.

2 Read R. A. Nicholson, P.72. & Ibn Hisham, *Sirat Rasul Allah*,PP.178-81.

therefore the first person who gave approval to Muhammad's prophetic claim.[1]

Islam—Beliefs and Practices

Fundamental Beliefs

- Allah is the one true God. He is not of the trinity. Christians, who believe in the trinity and say Jesus is God, are unbelievers and belong to hell for eternity (Q.9: 29-30; Q.66:9).
- The Qur'an is the most holy book on earth and supersedes other heavenly books.
- Muhammad is Allah's last messenger and his greatest prophet of all. Allah sent thousands of prophets and Muhammad is the seal of all.
- There are many angels and demons (jinns or bad angels). Gabriel is the head of good angels and Satan is the head of bad angels who deceive people. In the Qur'an, sometime bad angels do good things. They are called the servants of Allah, who serve Allah and prophets.
- There will be a judgment day, and only on that day will people be able to find out whether they go to heaven or hell.
- Allah has predetermined the destiny of everybody before creation, be it in heaven or hell. People's righteous deeds may or may not effect the decision of Allah. Therefore, no Muslim is sure of personal salvation.

Fundamental Practices

The practices in Islam are based on *Shari'a*, the Way or the Law of life in Islam. Shari'a derives it values from the Qur'an and traditions (*Sunnah*). Traditions are made of Muhammd's sayings and actions, and they are collected in the books that are named the Hadiths and the Sira of Muhammad. Qur'an calls Muhammad the best model for humanity, and for this

---

1 Ibn Hisham, *Sirat Rasul Allah,* PP.210-11.

reason, a committed Muslim is obliged to practice whatever Muhammad did or instructed Muslims to do:

Devotional Practices

- Praying five times daily (at sunrise, mid-day, mid-afternoon, sunset, and at night before retiring). In regard to prayer, Islam has followed an Arabian Jewish pattern of praying five times daily.[1] This also matches the Zoroastrian pattern of prayer that was mentioned in the previous chapter.
- Fasting in the month of Ramadan, which was the practice of Meccan pagans.
- The pilgrimage to Mecca, which is called *Haj*. All practices in the time of Haj are borrowed from pagans.
- Giving alms

Moral Practices

- Correcting people in the family and community by the Shari'a in order to protect the Islamic codes about concerning behavior, clothing and cover, appearance, forbidden things (*haraam*) and so forth.
- At family level, father or husband is a "governor" or "administrator" of the family to control his wife and children, even to employ violence, if necessary. The Qur'an says;

  > If any of your women are guilty of lewdness, Take the evidence of four witnesses from amongst you against them; and if they testify, confine them to houses until death do claim them, or Allah ordain for them some (other) way (Q.4:15).

- At state level, ruler must make sure that Islam permeates society at all levels, and the principles of Islam are in practice everywhere.

---

1 Louis A. Ginzberg, *A Commentary on the Palestinian Talmud*, New York, Vol. I, 1941, P.73.

Social Practices

- Instructions about men, women, non-Muslims, marriage, family, divorce, trade, slavery, evangelism, etc.

Judicial Practices

- Penalties and punishments such as lashing, hanging, stoning, amputations and others.

Life and Death in Islam

It is not easy to derive a clear statement regarding life and death in Islam. However, Muslims believe that:

- Life on earth is a period of examination in which every one prepares oneself for the life to come. The life in this world is a battleground between good and evil deeds. The predominance of good or evil deeds in this world will bring the relevant consequence after physical death - either eternal life or eternal death.

- Salvation or eternal life is based on continuous purification by good deeds in this world. Although each Muslim should try his or her best to be good, ultimately Allah himself will do the measuring at judgment day. Therefore in Islam there is no justification of sinners by faith as in Christianity, and no one, including Muhammad himself, is assured of personal salvation. The Qur'an says;

    No soul can know what it will earn tomorrow (Q.31:34).

- There will be a judgment day held in hell;

    So by the lord without doubt we (Allah) *shall gather them (righteous) together and also the evil ones with them, then shall we bring them forth on their knees round about Hell* (Q.19:67).

- Islamic people believe that God is just and will treat each according to one's deeds. However, they traditionally, and without either logic or deep consideration of this, say that God may ignore their sins and forgive them. Therefore in this way, there is a false and even a non-Islamic hope among Muslims that salvation can be granted after death.

Islam's heaven (paradise) is a garden with flowing streams, with beautiful greenery, fruits and maidens with beautiful, big and lustrous eyes for men (Q.2:25; Q.52:22-23; 44:51-55). For Muslim warriors there will also be young boys; they will be like scattered pearls of perpetual freshness with cups of flowing wine in their hands (Q.52:24; 56:17; 76:19).

These words were not introduced to Arabs by Allah (and Muhammad) for the first time. Like fasting in the month of Ramadan or walking seven times around Ka'ba (the central shrine in Mecca), they were taught in pre-Islamic era by pagans (and their god Allah) through poetry. Muhammad borrowed[1] all these practices from paganism probably to make his fellow Arabs happy that he had not come to reject the beliefs of his ancestors but to protect them under the worship of one god, Allah.

The New Faith Spreads

At the end of his first twelve years of ministry, Muhammad's preaching severely angered the people of Mecca - some of them even plotted to kill him. The people of Mecca felt his ministry was not only spiritually a threat to their most respected shrine, Ka'bah, they also saw it as a serious threat to their peaceful relationships and trades, which were principles they felt obliged to uphold in honor of the deities in Mecca. The most hostile tribe of Arabia towards Muhammad was convinced that any kind of violence was dishonoring to the deities in the Ka'bah. Therefore, the Ka'bah was like a safe haven for all Arabs spiritually, socially, politically and economically. This was the reason why they saw Muhammad's message as a threat to all aspects of their lives and, therefore, tried to block his progress.

---

1 Read R. A. Nicholson, P.167.

As mentioned previously, Muhammad fled to Medina where he was warmly welcomed by an Arabic tribe. He and his newly adapted tribe made raids on the Meccan caravans and this naturally encouraged hostility between them and his followers.[1] Ultimately, Muhammad and his followers made great wealth via this invasion, employed many fighters, returned to Mecca, occupied the city and forced the Meccans to accept Islam and to acknowledge him as a prophet.

After conquering Mecca and uniting the tribal leaders around him, Muhammad was heavily influenced by the Meccans. An outcome of this was that Muhammad became very nationalistic. He adopted some of the Arabic rituals that he had practiced before Islam. To satisfy the nationalistic desires of Arabs against Jews, he abandoned praying to Jerusalem and instructed Muslims to pray facing Mecca (Q.2:142-144). It was at this time that he chose Mecca to be the holy shrine and the focal religious place for Muslims.

The hatred towards the children of Israel was revived in Mecca at this time, even more intense than before the birth of Islam, since Jews did not see his claims in accord with the Bible and started to reject and ridicule Muhammad's claims.[2] Muhammad turned his sword against the Jews, Christians and pagans, killing many both openly and secretly[3] calling it the battle of God against unbelievers;

> *But when the forbidden months are past, then fight and slay the Pagans wherever you find them, an seize them, beleaguer*

---

1 Bukhari: Volume 7, Book 67, Hadith 402. & Muslim: Book 21, Hadith 4756. & Colin Chapman, Cross & Crescent, England, Inter Varsity Press, 1995, P.91.

2 W. E. Shephard, *Muslims Attitudes Toward Judaism and Christianity,* P. 2.

3 Read Tabari, Muhammad-bin Jarir, *Tarikh-al-rosol val-molouk,* PP.997-8,1006,1056-7. & Ibn Hisham, *Sirat Rasul Allah*, PP.491-3. & G. Nehls: quotations from the books of Sahih Muslim III PP.963-966.

them, and lie in wait for them in every stratagem (of war);
but if they repent, and establish regular prayers and practise
regular charity, then open the way for them: for Allah is Oft-
forgiving, Most Merciful. . . . Make war upon such of those
to whom the Scripture have been given as believe not in God,
or in the last day, and who forbid not that which God and
His Apostle have forbidden, and who profess not the profession
of the truth, until they pay tribute out of hand, and they be
humbled. The Jews say, 'Ezra (Ozair) is a son of God'; and
the Christians say, 'The Messiah is a son of God.' Such the
sayings in their mouths! They resemble the saying of Infidels
of old! God do battle with them! How are they misguided!
(Q.9:5, 29-30).

In order to conquer the whole peninsula of Arabia, Muhammad
took advantage of the many wars that occurred against various
tribes and imposed Islam on them. In this way, the war against
non-Muslims (*jihad*) became sacred in Islamic faith;

Verily Allah loves those who, as though they were a solid wall,
do battle for his cause in serried lines! (Q.61:4).

O prophet! make war on the infidels and hypocrites, and deal
rigorously with them. Hell shall be their abode! and wretched
the passage to it (Q.66:9).

Every Muslim by faith became obligated to take part in the war
against non-Muslims [Q.2:216,217,253; 4:71; 8:65; 9:93-94].

The spread of Islam into other nations began with the invasions
launched from Mecca and Medina. After Muhammad, his
successors also encouraged holy war (jihad) against non-
Muslims.

Muslims conquered large portions of the two existing Empires,
the Byzantine and the Persian, within a single decade. One
after another the nations of Israel, Syria, Mesopotamia, Egypt,
Iraq, and Iran were conquered with the power of the Muslims'
sword. Muslims continued conquering as many nations as they

could and built an Islamic empire that stretched from northern Spain to India.[1]

Muhammad's Political and Religious Thought

Before his emigration to Medina, the 'spirit of war' was silent in Muhammad despite all the pressures on him. But after he fled from Mecca to Medina and founded a stronger following there, he suddenly turned his assembly into a fighting group. He did this in order to prevail against his opposition in Mecca. His strategy was to first invade the Meccan caravans and then the city itself. Unlike the pagan Meccans who valued the month of Ramadan and would not initiate any war against their enemies in it, Muhammad ordered his followers to attack unarmed caravans even in the so-called sacred month of Ramadan (Q.2:217)[2].

Medina was geographically well placed between Mecca and the Mediterranean world to cut the caravan route, which was of vital importance to Meccans' lives.[3] Under Muhammad's leadership, Muslims made much plunder from the raiding of caravans and from the battlefield.[4] One fifth of everything that was gained in war belonged to Muhammad, his families, orphans and the poor. The remaining four-fifths was to be divided among the warriors.[5] This encouraged Muslims to take revenge for what the Meccans had previously done to Muhammad and his

---

1 F. Quilici, *Children of Allah,* USA: Chartwell Books Inc., 1978, P.70. & C. Chapman, P.9.

2 This verse of the Qur'an contradicts the verse Q.9:5 which does not encourage war and killing in Ramadan.

3 J. B. Glubb, PP.34-35.

4 Read: Muhammad-bin Jarir Tabari, *Tarikh-al-rosol val-molouk,* PP.933-40,944,945, 950,1007.

5 Ibid, P.998. & V. Bailey, PP.18-19.

followers. In this way, the warlike spirit of pagan Bedouins[1] was not rejected by Muslims, but instead revived by Muslims more than ever before. Muhammad used the Bedouin strategy to empower the decision of his followers to fight and to gain the victory. The explosive force of the nomad world was linked to the preaching of Muhammad and a relationship of mutual help and dependence developed.[2] This mutual dependency gained power for Muhammad and prosperity in the form of wealth and possessions for his followers. The political aspirations and decisions of Muhammad and his companions were offered to the community as the inspired verses of God, which could not be reversed or rejected. Any one, who wanted to live, had to live as a Muslim. People did not have any other choice but to join Islam. They were forced to pronounce their allegiance to Muhammad and become Muslim by saying the Islamic creed:

There is no deity except Allah, and Muhammad is the messenger of Allah.

The atmosphere that Muhammad created was quite different to what Jesus created for people. Jesus, unlike Muhammad, offered a journey of thought that brought people into a dramatically different way of living and thinking from the way they were accustomed.[3] The spirit of war that was upon the people in Medina did not allow them the time to take Muhammad's preaching into their inner beings and evaluate them. Who was able to speak logic with the sword? People were so caught up with the rush and force of war that they did not have the chance to think or evaluate. Therefore, the people in Medina failed to consciously evaluate whether the verses of the Qur'an could be attributed to God or not. However, some people realized the problem and started blaming Muhammad. Muhammad took their criticism as a real threat to Islam and therefore launched a

---

1 K. Savage, *The History of World Religions,* London: The Bodley Head, 1970, P.118.

2 F. Quilici, P.68.

3 Read R. Zacharias, PP.29,46.

systematic plan to exterminate his critics from society. People had no choice other than to obey him because the Qur'an stipulated that his commands were to be considered as equal to God's commands (Q.33:36).

The Cause of Disinterest in Islam

Clearly, Muhammad was himself the cause of some of the criticisms that people made against him. His unstable beliefs expressed in the Qur'an (or the new religion) led to critiques being raised against him. On one hand he said that the followers of other religions need not feel saddened by the prospect of hell because no fear will come upon them. On the other hand, he expresses a contradictory attitude when he claims that Islam is the one and only. Examine the following passages;

> *Verily, they who believe* (Muslims)*, and they who follow the Jewish religion, and the Christians, and the Sabeites - whoever of these believeth in God and the last day, and doeth which is right, shall have their reward with their Lord: fear shall not come upon them, neither shall they be grieved* (Q.2:62).

On another occasion, he said that the book given to Moses was complete and was a means through which people could meet their Lord;

> *Then gave we* (God) *the Book to Moses - complete for him who should do right, and decision for matters, and guidance, and mercy, that they might believe in the meeting with their Lord* (Q.6:154).

People could say: if the followers of other religions have been freed from fear and if the book given to Moses is complete and perfect, and lifts the fallen people up to the presence of their Lord, why will they be in need of a new religion?

At another stage in his life, Muhammad said that he is not an upstart among the messengers of Israel, but the one who testifies something similar to what the children of Israel testified;

> *...I am no apostle of new doctrines...this book[1] be from God... its conformity with the Law* (Q.46:9-10).

This statement of doctrinal similarities, of course, was not confirmed by Jews and Christians who knew the central theme of their books, the Old and New Testaments. After migration from Mecca to Medina, Muhammad distanced himself from the church fully and relied more on pagan and Gnostic beliefs, which were in favor of his Arab friends and against Christians and Jews. In pre-Islamic era, people in Saudi Arabia had freedom to criticize ideas and people. Therefore, Christians and Jews took advantage of this freedom and started rejecting or even mocking Muhammad for his contradictory beliefs, as the Qur'an even records;

> *...they said, 'This is manifest sorcery!'* (Q.61: 6).

Either Muhammad's exaltation of idols at one time (as was mentioned earlier in this section) or his own doubts about the Qur'an could also have been cause for people to ridicule him. As a result, Muhammad started to doubt in his own religion and this further discouraged people to join his movement;

> *And if thou* (Muhammad) *art in doubt as to what we have sent down to thee, inquire at those who have read the Scriptures before thee. Now hath the truth come unto thee from thy Lord: be not therefore of those who doubt. Neither be of those who charge the signs of God with falsehood, lest thou be of those who perish* (Q.10:94-95).

The pressure of multiple opponents brought Muhammad to such a point that he intended to give up Islam. He reflected to others that the reason for this was his doubt in Islam. Therefore, his own decision to give up Islam and his doubts about Islam would certainly have caused many people to be disinterested in Islam and as a result to ridicule his lack of confidence in his own religion. But then a radical change occurred in him. Soon afterward, when he gained power, he forced people to

---

1 The Qur'an.

come to Islam and killed those who did not come to believe in it. This is the saddest and the most painful part of humanity. How tragic when people must be sacrificed because of a leader's uncertainty!

As further evidence of this uncertainty, look at what Muhammad said about Christians. On one hand he said the followers of Jesus Christ are ahead of unbelievers until the day of resurrection and in this way he indirectly guided Christians to stick to their religion and stay firm in their faith;

> … *God said,…I will place those who follow thee* (Jesus) *above those who believe not, until the day of resurrection* (Q.3:55).

On the other hand, he forced them to believe in Islam and to follow him;

> *Make war upon such of those to whom the Scriptures have been given as believe not in God, or in the last day, and who forbid not that which God and His Apostle have forbidden, and who profess not the profession of the truth, until they pay tribute out of hand, and they be humbled…The Jews say, 'Ezra is a son of God'; and the Christians say, 'the Messiah is a son of God.'…God do battle with them! How are they misguided* (Q.9:29-30).

Why would a Christian nation, who has overcome the sin of disbelief, be forced to change their faith? Isn't the victory over disbelief called the victory over Satan? If there was no doubt that Christians were winners through Jesus Christ, why would they leave their victorious King and come to join Muhammad who had no assurance in his own ministry? Needless to say, the unstable and shifting position held by Muhammad has caused severe havoc for Christians ever since the beginning of political Islam.

Muhammad killed many people, expelled the Jewish tribes from Medina, and seized all their property.[1] The forefathers of these Jews had fled from Roman persecution in Jerusalem centuries ago.[2] Through the centuries of hard work, their generations had built their lives in Medina, surviving the ages of violence, lawlessness and idolatry in the Peninsula of Arabia.[3] Obviously, the town of Medina owed much of its prosperity to the highly skilled Jewish inhabitants.[4] However, it is distressing to see that under the government of the so-called civilized Islam they were not even given a chance to live. In one of his attacks on the last Jewish tribe in Medina, Muhammad called the Jews the sworn enemies of Allah, killed all the men of the tribe and sold the woman and children into slavery.[5] He said to his followers: *If you gain a victory over the men of Jews, kill them.*[6] Also, those of his opponents, who escaped and took refuge in Mecca, were killed or forced to accept Islam by Muhammad when he later captured Mecca. So, in this way, the prophetic calling of Muhammad turned into a dictatorship with many battles and the shedding of blood occurring after his emigration to Medina.

---

1 Read: Muhammad-bin Jarir Tabari, *Tarikh-al-rosol val-molouk*, PP. 997,998,1006,1056-7. & Ibn Hisham, *Sirat Rasul Allah*, PP.491-3. & W.M. Watt, *Muhammad at Medina*, Oxford: Clarendon Press, 1956,P.14-16. & M.H. Haykal, *The Life of Muhammad*, Indianapolis: North American Trust Publications, 1976, P.243-4,278. & J. B. Glubb, PP.35-36.

2 P. W. Crittenden, P.4. & K. Savage, PP.124-5.

3 Muslims call the pre-Islamic Arabs ignorant (jahil), lawless, violent and idolaters (J. R. Hinnells, P. 168 & R. El Droubie, P.5).

4 P. W. Crittenden, P.4.

5 Bukhari, Volume 5, Book 58, Hadith 148. & T. Andrae, *Muhammad: The Man and His Faith*, New York: Harper & Row Publishers, 1955, PP.155-6.

6 Davud, Book 19, Hadith 2996.

The One Community of Hezballah

After his emigration, it was not a kind of theology that ran the course of Islam but a fighting and fluctuating spirit against flesh and blood, although Islam carried with itself various religious rituals too. This agenda was driven by a conviction that 'the region must be conquered by the sword' in order to rescue the world from corruption;

> ...*and were it not for the restraint of one by means of the other, imposed on men by God, verily the earth had been utterly corrupted* (Q.2:251b).

In this way, Islam became the first and last religion ever in the history of humankind that believed so extremely in erasing the believers of other religions at all times and in all places. Indeed, the harshest pre-Islamic cultural values were all gathered from the various tribal values and united into, what seems to be, a single tribe of Islam, Hezballah, which must overcome all other so-called corrupt groups. In other words, the habits and cultural values of the conquerors became the dominant and authoritative forces over the region. All tribes were forced in absolute dedication to Muhammad as the chief of the new politico-religious movement, which meant no one had freedom of choice in any of their affairs. He decreed:

> *It is not fitting for a Believer, man or woman, when a matter has been decided by Allah and His Apostle to have any option about their decision: if any one disobeys Allah and His Apostle, he is indeed on a clearly wrong Path* (Q.33:36).

Contrary to his earlier ministry in Mecca as a Warner only, Muhammad established a theocratic system that let him to force people to bow down to Islam and shed the blood of those who rejected his call.[1] While he was in contact with the church in his earlier ministry in Mecca, he relied very much on a prophetic culture, which was a calling of people to fear the true God. Contrary to his earlier ministry, his later

---

1 N. Anderson, P.95.

ministry became predominantly legal and political, and he relied on forcing people to follow him. He invaded tribes by the thousands and forced them to follow him as the head of the state religion. In his earlier ministry, he was harmless to idol worshipers and friendly to every one who believed in one God. However, in his later ministry he called any who did not follow him an enemy, no matter if the person had faith in one God or many gods. It was from this time that many contradictions in the verses of the Qur'an began to appear.

After his emigration to Medina, everybody had to please Muhammad by giving up his/her religion and following his instructions. This was because he was no longer a rejected prophet like in Mecca, but a powerful political figure with the goal of turning the various religious and cultural ethnicities in the Peninsula of Arabia into a single community of Islam, Hezballah.

If someone, for any possible reason, did not live to please the prophet of Allah, he/she would be brought face to face with the sword. The authority he laid over his people was even more than a contemporary Bedouin chief possessed over his tribe.[1]

So, in this way, the growing doctrine of Islam became influenced by the Muslim strategy of non-stop invasions of other peoples and tribes;

> ...*kill those who join other gods with God wherever ye shall find them: and seize them, besiege them, and lay wait for them with every kind of ambush: but if they shall convert, and observe prayer, and pay the obligatory alms, then let them go their way, for God is gracious, Merciful* (Q.9:5).

Invasions and forcing people to believe in Islam became the climactic issue of Muslim doctrine. In order to make the growing body of doctrine convincing Muhammad welcomed all sorts of ideas that could give the movement a religious flavor. This kind of politics, especially when it is accompanied

---

1 P. W. Crittenden, P.12.

by force, has always been convincing to nominal people under threat, throughout history. When people see themselves face to face with death, more often they prefer to choose life with whatever conditions the dominant power imposes on them. This was what happened in the Arabian Peninsula as well. Muhammad and his companions forcefully convinced people that his invasions were God's will and ought to be accepted as an expression of irreversible religious values. Therefore, Islamic doctrine couldn't help but contain the words and acts of a group of fighting warriors and this was presented to others as the absolute law that must be obeyed and honored. Thus, a fighting spirit became the leading characteristic in producing the doctrine of Islam. The battles against Meccans turned into battles against non-Muslims and ultimately swept through entire societies that were full of a variety of people, including Christians and Jews.

Muhammad's views became subject to the enormous growth in his political power and this is seen clearly in the changing ethics applied in the treatment of Jews and Christians. The Qur'an clearly reveals two opposite views about Jews and Christians that were held at different times. The verses of his early ministry were apparently in favor of Jews and Christians and consequently in favor of biblical theology, but the verses after his emigration were against the followers of the Bible and thus contrary to biblical theology. After the death of Muhammad, many Muslim jurists acknowledged the changes in his attitudes but accepted them as Allah's decision in allowing the latter verses of Qur'an cancel the authority of the earlier verses. [1]

Instability in Friendship

When a doctrine becomes subject to war, it undoubtedly contradicts itself in many ways. A fighting spirit always searches

---

1 Abu al-Kasim Hibat-Allah Ibn Salama, *An-Nasikh wal-Mansukh*, Cairo: Dar al-Ma'arif, 1966, PP. 4-5, 123. Abrogated verses are listed on PP.142-3. See also PP.7, 11, 26-7, 37, 46. & John Burton, *The Encyclopedia of Islam*, Vol.7. S.V. "Naskh." P.1010.

for full armor and empowerment, no matter what it will cost the community. This is the major aim in fighting. To do so, the warring authorities sometimes decide to stay in favor with a particular group and out of favor with another. Subsequently, though, because of a change in war policy, they change their strategy and become friends with their previous enemy in order to crush their previous friend. Such an unstable spirit always ends up opposing its own doctrine in many areas. That is why the Qur'an contradicts itself so many times. For example, in regard to the prophetic role of Muhammad Allah states that Muhammad's ministry is not to lead people but to call them in a peaceful manner, since man is alert and able to distinguish the good from bad. On the other hand, Allah commands Muhammad to fight people and frighten them until they come to Islam and offer their allegiance to it (cf. Q.76:2-3; 2:272; 3:19-20,110; 22:49; 9:29).

In this way, the so-called theocratic law of Islam imposed on people an unstable standard, in which people could lie and deceive for the sake of Allah. As a result, lying, treachery and deception became Islam's key tactics in conquering others. These tactics are gathered in a doctrinal statement called Taqiyya (*Taghiyya*) which is one of the most efficient arms for the spread of Islam. It means "Holy Deception" which means use every lie you can in order to spread Islam or win the war against the enemy.

Islam's Holy Deception not only threatened the life of non-Muslims, but Muslims also were not able to ever hope for a long-term friendly relationship with each other.

This bitter, fearful, painful and hopeless instability cannot be attributed to the loving and merciful God who desires and calls people back to heaven as the place of peace and honest relationships.[1]

---

1 Read the Gospel of Jesus Christ.

41

The instability of relationships in Islamic politics has reduced the level of sincere mutual trust among people and as a result has caused many to spy on one another in fundamentalist Islamic societies. Many force themselves into a situation where they have to be two-faced. This unrealistic life sometimes penetrates into the inner world of families and of immediate friends, bringing with it many unfortunate results. For example, the disagreement between the successors of Muhammad and the war between Muhammad's beloved wife, Aisha, and his beloved son-in-law, Ali, were the result of Muhammad's own fluctuating values with respect to relationships. The members of his own family and state became a threat to each other.

In this way, sincere family fellowships were changed into an impossible situation for many. Even mothers, who are known to be a source of shelter and trust for their children, became yet another threat to the members of their family. After the Revolution of 1979, several mothers were rewarded by the Islamic Republic of Iran as being pure Muslims when they surrendered their children for the crime of following other Islamic leaders rather than the Ayatollah Khomeini.

Interest in Pagan Objects

Muhammad originally had Christian companions. Later on, people who had previously opposed him became his companions as they desired a religion that was oriented around and for Arabs. The Christian thought that was once honored by Muhammad was no longer suited to his new surroundings. Now pagan religious rituals were to be adopted and incorporated into Islam;

> *Verily, Safa and Marwah are among the monuments of God: whoever then maketh a pilgrimage to the temple, or visiteth it, shall not be to blame if he go round about them both...* (Q.2:158; cf. 22:26-27).

The hills of Safa and Marwah in the above verse are in the sacred territory of Mecca, and these had been the objects of pagan worship.[1]

In the early years of his ministry, Muhammad had no interest in the objects of pagan faith. However, the pro-Arabic nature of his later ministry not only resulted in the revival and legitimization of some of these pagan rituals[2], but he also called Jews and Christians, who believed in One God, to leave their biblical path and instead follow his newly adopted path. Although his path became quite different to that of Moses and Jesus, he still wanted Christians and Jews to make no distinction between himself and other prophets. Those who did make a distinction and even those who desired to take a middle way were all made subject to shameful punishment;

> *Of a truth they who believe not on God and his Apostles, and seek to separate God from his Apostles, and say, 'Some we believe, and some we believe not,' and desire to take a middle way; These! they are veritable infidels! and for the infidels have we prepared a shameful punishment. And they who believe on God and his Apostles, and make no difference between them - these! we will bestow on them their reward at last. God is Gracious, Merciful* (Q.4:150-152).

People were not given any freedom to compare and choose the best belief that represents a high quality of life and faith. Instead, blind submission, obedience and allegiance became

---

1 Read the note number 62 in THE KORAN, translated by J. M. Rodwell, London: Everyman, 1994, P.435.

2 Muhammad sanctified and dedicated the ancient pagan shrine, Ka'bah, to Allah and Islamised the pilgrimage of 'Hajj' to it. The pilgrimage of 'Hajj' was one of the most respected pagan rites and he made it the 'fifth' pillar of his religion (Read Tabari, Muhammad-bin Jarir, *Commentary on the Qur'an,* P.1771. & H. Thomas, *An Unfinished History of the World,* London: Hamish Hamilton, 1979, P.145. & K. Armstrong, P.182 & K. Savage, P.125 & B. W. Sharratt, P.76).

the lasting focal points of Islam. Everyone was forced to confess faith in Muhammad. This led Muslims after Muhammad to build their theological foundation simply on the two rigid confessions, "there is no god except Allah, and Muhammad is his messenger". These two statements were announced to the world, not for open evaluation and selection but as forceful "gifts" from Islam requiring blind submission by the world. Any act of objecting to Muhammad was taken as an objection against God and therefore carried the death penalty with it. According to Islam, if Allah has revealed that Muhammad's will must be done on earth, then how could the people of the world dare to ignore or oppose his will?

2

The Author of the Qur'an

Compiling the Original Qur'an

A Question of Authenticity

Compiling the Original Qur'an

Muhammad's associates preserved his teachings by memorizing or writing them down during his lifetime. Later, the materials of his teaching were collected and made into a book, called "the Qur'an" (Koran). The word "*Qur'an*" or "*Ghur'an*," means "*reading aloud or recitation*" and is derived from the Arabic root "*qara'a*" or "*ghara'a*," meaning "*to read*." The first word "*eqra* or *eghra* (the command form of the verb "*read*") that Muhammad heard from an angel might have been one of the reasons for Muslims to name the book of their religion *Qur'an*," which is from the same root as "*eqra*."

Muslims believe that the Qur'an is the collected pre-existent, eternal and authoritative words of God conveyed by the angel Gabriel to Muhammad, in order to be recited in Arabic to Arabs. They believe that it is God's full, final and supreme revelation given to Muhammad throughout some twenty-three years of his ministry:

> *Elif. Lam. Ra. These are signs of the clear Book. An Arabic Koran have we sent it down, that ye might understand it* (Q.12:1-2).

> *Ha, Mim. By the Luminous Book! We have made it an Arabic Koran that ye may understand. And it is a transcript of the archetypal Book, kept by us; it is lofty, filled with wisdom* (Q.43:1-4).

> *Recite thou, in the name of thy Lord who create; Created man from CLOTS OF BLOOD; Recite thou! For thy Lord is the most Beneficent, Who hath taught the use of pen; Hath taught Man that which he knoweth not* (Q.96:1-5).

> *SAY: whoso is the enemy of Gabriel - For he (Gabriel) is who by God's leave hath caused (the Qur'an) to descend on thy (Muhammad's) heart, the confirmation of previous*

revelations, and guidance, and good tidings to the faithful (Q.2:97).

The word "recite" in Q.96:1 means the recitation of those words that were already written and existed.

For Muslims, the Qur'an supersedes any other religious books in the world. According to Islamic faith, no one else's thoughts, including Muhammad's, could be reflected in the Qur'an, because it is a copy of the original Qur'an, which was written in eternity and is in heaven:

> *... with Him* (Allah) *is the source of revelation*[1] (Q.13:39).

> *Thou didst not recite any book (of revelation) before it: with that right hand of thine thou didst not transcribe one: else might they who treat it as a vain thing have justly doubted: But it is a clear sign in the hearts of those whom "the knowledge" hath reached. None except the wicked reject our signs* (Q.29:48-49).

> *Yet it is a glorious Koran, Written on the preserved Table* (Q.85:21-22).

A Question of Authenticity

However, the Qur'an's own verses and Islam's own ancient authentic sources[2] do not support it as being the pre-existent, eternal and the authoritative word of God. Credence is given to the contribution of other writers to the Qur'an, as many verses in the Qur'an are not inspired through Muhammad but are from his companions.[3]

---

1 In Arabic, the "source of revelation" is "*Om*-al-Kitab," which literally means "the Mother of the Book" or the Qur'an.

2 For example, Muhammad-bin Jarir Tabari, *Tarikh-al-rosol val-molouk*, P.882. & Muhammad-bin Jarir Tabari, *Commentary on the Qur'an*, PP.1769-71.

3 A. Dashti, *Twenty Three Years*, London: George Allen & Unwin, 1985, PP.98,111.

The present Qur'an was also called incomplete and different from other rival versions and was accepted as false by many eyewitnesses of Muhammad—even by Muhammad's own son-in-law, Ali, the first holy leader (Imam) of the sect of Shia.[1]

According to the old authorities and Hadiths[2] of Islam, there were many disagreements among the contemporary followers of Muhammad over the wordings and readings of the Qur'anic verses. Muhammad himself became uncertain and could not recognize the original words and readings. Therefore, he ordered his followers to follow whatever scriptures each one had, regardless of the differences in the meanings and versions.[3]

He had also claimed that the Qur'an cannot be inspired by anyone besides Allah:

> *And if ye be in doubt as to that which we have sent down to our servant, then produce a Sura* [chapter] *like it, and summon your witnesses, beside God, if ye are men of truth: But if ye do it not, and never shall ye do it, then fear the fire prepared for the infidels, whose fuel is men and stones* (Q.2:23-24).

> *Can they not consider the Koran? Were it from any other than God, they would surely have found in it many contradictions* (Q.4:82).

> *Moreover this Koran could not have been devised by any but God.... Do they say, "He hath devised it himself?" SAY: Then*

---

1 G. Nehls, PP. 52-55.

2 Hadiths are the writings about Muhammad's and his companions' sayings and deeds, which guide Muslims in founding their social laws and governments, and also in conducting their daily lives (cf. Q.4:80; 7:157; 14:44;33:21). Sometimes Muslims regard the writings of the Hadiths on a conditional basis. They do not welcome those parts of the Hadiths that represent contradictions. To evade the contradictions, they rely instead on their own notions. However, without referring to Hadiths, Muslims are not able to discover the original context of the words spoken by Muhammad: the time and the occasion they relate to.

3 G. Nehls, PP. 57-65.

> *bring a Sura like it; and call on whom ye can beside God, if ye speak truth* (Q.10:37-38).

> *SAY: Verily, were men and Djinn[1] assembled to produce the like of this Koran, they could not produce its like, though the one should help the other* (Q.17:88).

Muhammad again had claimed that the Qur'an was an inspired revelation to him with the full knowledge of Allah. He purported that Allah and his angels were witnesses to this, and none could change it, and that he was merely a mouthpiece for the inspired words of Allah:

> *But God is himself witness of what he hath sent down to thee: In His knowledge hath He sent it down to thee. The angels are also witnesses: but God is a sufficient witness* (Q.4:166).

> *Before thee have apostles already been charged with falsehood: but they bore the charge and the wrong with constancy, till our help came to them; for none can change the words of God.... And the words of thy Lord are perfect in truth and in justice: none can change his words: He is the hearing, knowing* (Q.6:34,115).

> *For them are good tidings in this life, and in the next! There is no change in the words of God! This is the great felicity* (Q.10:64).

> *Will they say, "He hath devised It?" SAY: If I have devised the Koran, then not one single thing shall ye ever obtain from God! He best knoweth what ye utter in its regard! Witness enough is He between me and you! And He is the Gracious, the Merciful. SAY: I am no apostle of new doctrines: neither know I what will be done with me or you. Only what is revealed to me do I follow, and I am only charged to warn openly* (Q.46:8-9).

Yet Muhammad introduced himself as an authoritative figure, able to abrogate Allah's verses in the Qur'an. He states in some areas of the Qur'an that his verses are better than those of

---

1 Spirits.

Allah and therefore he substitutes his own "better" or "similar" verses:[1]

> *Whatever verses we cancel, or cause thee to forget, we bring a better or its like. Knowest thou not that God hath power over all things?... Would ye ask your apostle what of old was asked of Moses? But he who exchangeth faith for unbelief, has already erred from the even way* (Q.2:106,108).

> *And when we change one verse for another, and God knoweth best what He revealeth, they say, "Thou art only a fabricator." Nay! But most of them have no knowledge* (Q.16:101).

> *Will they say, He hath forged it? Nay, it is the truth from the Lord that thou mayest warn a people to whom no warner has come before thee, that haply they may be guided* (Q.32:3).

This substitution caused Muhammad's contemporaries to accuse him of slandering God. People mainly accused him because of his own claim that the Qur'an could not be inspired or changed by anyone.

Among Muhammad's associates, there were some enslaved scholars from different nations, who were released from slavery by Muhammad and joined his movement. Muhammad was not familiar with the languages of other religions and so he had no easy access to them. The other religions were open to him only through his foreign associates. After Muhammad's immigration to Medina, even some of his own followers realized that he was using the statements of other religions and poets as his own and as the verses of the Qur'an. Some of them left him as a sign of criticism and run away in order to secure their lives. The following qur'anic verse proves that a large number of people in Arabia knew of his heavy reliance on enslaved scholars from other religions and he had no choice but to publicly defend himself:

---

1 To find the verses that Muhammad substituted with Allah's verses, read Abu al-Kasim Hibat-Allah Ibn Salama, PP. 142-3. & Gerhard Nehls, *Christians Ask Muslims*, PP. 11-15.

We, also know that they say, "Surely a certain person teacheth him [Muhammad]*." But the tongue of him at whom they hint is foreign[1], while this Koran is in the plain Arabic* (Q.16:103).

It is because of this foreign influence that there are parts of the Qur'an that strongly resemble different traditions and literature from other religions and beliefs. The Qur'an contains many themes that appear in the Old Testament, New Testament, Apocrypha, Talmud (Haggadah), and the Avesta—the book of Zoroastrians.[2] One example—Jesus Christ as "the Word and the Spirit of God"—is taken from the New Testament although it does not fit with the theology of Islam. Another example is the idea of the *bridge of sirat*[3] ("Chinvat" or "Chinvad" in Zoroastrianism), that finds its origin in Zoroastrian belief.[4]

---

1   The actual word for "foreign" in Arabic is *"A'jami,"* that refers to the language of Salman Parsi, which is Farsi or Persian.

2   R. B. Smith, *Mohammed and Mohammedanism,* London, 1889, P.146. & J. Gilchrist, *The Textual History of the Qur'an and the Bible,* Reprinted by WEC International, 1987, PP.34-6. & H. J. Heydt, *A Comparison of World Religions,* Pennsylvania: Christian Literature Crusade, 1976, P.66. & R. Machatschke, P.1. & G. Nehls, P.100-101.

3   Allah sets the *bridge of sirat* over hell. The pathway of the bridge is sharp like a sword or thin like a string of hair. Only Muslims who are more dedicated will be able to cross this bridge and enter paradise. Those who cannot cross the bridge are the condemned people. They will fall into the fiery lake of hell. According to Islamic traditions, Muhammad can turn this impossible situation into possibility for the condemned dead people if they call for Muhammad's intercession.

4   Yasna1 (19:6), P.208 and Yasna2, P.201. The Vendidad (book2) translation by Hashem Razi, in Persian, 1997 (1376), P. 831. & Khordeh Avesta, edited by Rashid Shahmardan, Bombay-India: Published by P. P. Bharucha, Hon. Secy, The Iranian Zoroastrian Anjuman, 1929 (1308), P.177. Also see J. R. Hinnells, *Zoroastrianism and the Parsis, P.10,32. &* E. G. Parrinder, *A Book of World Religions,* P.115.

For hundreds of years before the rise of Islam, the Jews brought about a remarkable change in the religious lives of the Arab people. Their customs and traditions were known to and practiced by many Arabs.[1] This may be one of the reasons for the Apostle Paul's journey to Arabia (Galatians 1:17).

Many verses in the Qur'an, Muhammad's biography and his comments in the Hadiths (books of Islamic traditions) all prove that Muhammad was almost Judaized. It is in this way that the Qur'an owes a tremendous debt to the Hebrew writings and traditions. However, the Qur'an is not drawn so much from the written but the oral Jewish law and traditions which grew around it.[2] It was because of Muhammad's illiteracy that he was not able to lean on the written scriptures of other religions but rather had to rely on the traditions or the word of mouth of his associates. His borrowing from other oral religious traditions may be a contributing factor in Islamic superstition, as oral tradition may be tainted by superstition.

A comparison between the Qur'an's material with other contemporary religious traditions and writings certainly proves that Muhammad has borrowed a lot of the Qur'an's materials from them.[3]

Muhammad was fully aware of the importance of Judaism in the Arabian Peninsula. For this reason he could not avoid it and leaned heavily upon it while also using both Christian[4] and Zoroastrian traditions for the advancement of his new structure.[5] He traced his own genealogy to Abraham through

---

1 A. I. Katsh, *Judaism and the Koran,* New York: A. S. Barnes and Company, Inc., 1962, Introduction.

2 R. B. Smith, P. 46.

3 Ch. C. Torrey, *The Jewish Foundation of Islam,* New York: 1933, P. 61.

4 Colin Chapman, PP. 114-115.

5 We know from the Qur'an that Muhammad's contemporaries accused him of being taught by someone (Q.16:103).

his son Ishmael, saying that God could not omit the Arabs from the revelations with which He favored the Arabs' cousins, the Jews and the Christians.

Muhammad believed that both the Torah and the New Testament had writings about him (Q.7: 157; 61:6). He considered himself the seal of all the prophets:

> *Muhammad is not the father of any man among you, but he is the Apostle of God, and the seal of the prophets: and God knoweth all things* (Q.33: 40).

However, the Qur'an, along with the Bible, states that the prophetic line has come from the house of Isaac and Jacob, not Ishmael, the forefather of Muhammad (Q.29:27).

Muhammad also considered Islam superior to all religions:

> *He it is who hath sent His Apostle with the Guidance and a religion of the truth, that He make it victorious over every other religion, albeit they who assign partners to God be averse from it* (Q.9: 33).

One reason for Muslims calling the Qur'an the highest and the greatest compared with the New Testament and Old Testament is their belief that the Qur'an came down through one human instrument, whereas the Bible came down via many prophets. They believe too that the author of the Bible is God and the original manuscripts are in heaven. Muslims totally reject the authorship of the books of God by any man. They believe that the Bible and the Qur'an came down as a verbal transmission from heaven and the prophets are only the bearers of the words of God.

Contrary to this, we are told in the Bible that God called, informed, enabled and inspired many humans as instruments to reveal His will so that it could be related to others' thoughts and hearts and make sense to them. God's revelation must be interlinked with human experience and history in order to make sense. The Bible says that the Word and the Spirit of

God became flesh and was the body of Jesus Christ, the Son. The title "Son" means the Word and the Spirit of God came to share in the lives of humankind in order to make the difference between eternal life and death understandable, and to make salvation holistic, applicable to mind, body, soul and spirit (Hebrews 2:14-17).

So the belief that the Qur'an was written in eternity and is pre-existent means that it has come into being apart from human experience and outside a natural historical development. Therefore, it is irrelevant to history and man's life. In the same way, the words "revelation," "inspiration," "prophecy," "apostle," "messenger" or "be righteous," which are mentioned in the Qur'an, do not make sense for a person of history if the Qur'an is written in eternity where there was no man. In the Bible, history started by the revelation of God's words in and since creation, by His personal revelation to Adam and Eve and by His words of instructions to them.

3

Misinformation by Muslim Evangelists

Introduction

The Failure of Christian Witness

Incomplete Religions

The Bible—Accurate or Altered?

The Qur'an—Complete Revelation from God?

Three Gods?

Teachers Equal with God?

Teaching on Acceptance or Religious Discrimination

Introduction

Muslim misinformation about Christianity is a product of the political, economic and social factors present at the time of the rise of Islam. Islam as a political religion legitimized political control over all aspects of life, in order to turn the diverse tribes of the Arabian Peninsula into one Muslim community. To reach other nations, they chose a forceful, one-way political view with no right of free choice for other nations: the only choice was to accept Islam. Because of Islam's absolutist approach, those who did not accept Islam were introduced to Muslims as those who were ignorant (*Jahil* in Arabic) and in error for rejecting Muhammad as the seal of prophets. The Christians of Muhammad's time also were not exempt from these types of thoughts and accusations when it came to evangelism. This teaching created the doctrine of hatred in Islam toward others, including Christians.

The best way to overcome this tragedy that has so harmed the relationship between Muslims and Christians right from the beginnings of Islam, is to study the words of the Qur'an and the Bible. These two books need to be compared by considering a great question. The question is "How can humankind get rid of hatred of any kind, including religious hatred, and thereby unite with one another on the basis of heavenly peace?"

This chapter touches the basis of several areas of misinformation by Muslim evangelists concerning Christianity.

The Failure of Christian Witness

The failure of Christians when it came to following the standards of Christ drew a wrong picture of the Christian faith in the minds of Muhammad and his friends. The church in Mecca was more in the service of the Roman Empire than in the service of Jesus Christ. This, of course, was not a problem for Muhammad at the beginning of his relationship with the church when he was attending the church and did not have strong pagan oppositions in Mecca. He was happy, the church was happy, especially when he found a job and eventually a wife through the church. However, the problem started later when his wife, Khadijah, and the priest of the church, Nofel, died and the church became totally absent in his life when he was face to face with the pagan's harsh attitudes and death threats. He may have expected the church, the servant of the great empire, to give him a strong shelter or find a secure place for him to take refuge, but we see something different happened. Some of his friends escaped and took refuge in the country of Ethiopia and he himself escaped to Medina and took refuge in a tribe that was anti-Jews and anti-Christians and dependant on looting caravan.

Christians failed to teach Muhammad the real faith in Christ. Muhammad was not aware of the central message of the Bible and of what Christ did on the Cross for the salvation of Muhammad and his country people. The church's whole effort was to see the Peninsula one day fallen into the hands of Roman Empire through conversion. Now, not only this hope was vanished but some of its attendees, including Muhammad, also were expelled from his homeland, Mecca. This failure brought great disappointments into Muhammad's life. Such a failure could become a great excuse for a tribe that hated Christians and Jews and gave shelter to Muhammad. After his immigration, Muhammad never ceased his criticism of Christians, whom he praised for years while he was in Mecca.

What Muslims heard from Muhammad's mouth was taken as sufficient proof for rejecting the Christian faith. What they saw from the traditions and religious lives of those living in Christian society, they perceived as something portrayed in the pages of the Bible. The Bible did not exist in Arabic so that people could discover the truth in it. Because of their lack of knowledge about the Bible, they were not able to distinguish the difference between carnal, contemporary "Christian" lives and the life led by the Spirit of the Bible. They assumed they were the same. Year after year Muslims without knowledge neglected and ignored the Bible more than ever. They adapted their faith and movement so that it took on a nature of bigotry, causing a major rift between Muslims and Christians.

The accusations of Muslims against the Christian faith have remained out of touch with the words of Jesus Christ ever since the rise of Islam as a political religion after the immigration of Muhammad to Medina. Many times, we have heard fanatical Muslims on radio, TV, in taxis and in their newspapers accusing Christians of killing Muslims in the Crusades, in Bosnia, etc. Whilst concluding Christianity is to blame, they show ignorance of the words of Jesus Christ, from whom Christianity originated, who says, *"our struggle is not against flesh and blood but against the spiritual forces of evil"* (Ephesians 6:12).

Muslims do not know that Jesus' philosophy is to love all humankind, no matter what their situation, and to hate Satan. Jesus sacrificed Himself for all humanity in order to release them from the clutches of Satan. Muslims do not know that the love of Jesus Christ, the Son of the Almighty God, is for Christians, Muslims, Jews, the godly, the godless; in short, for the entire universe. For Him no one nation is better than the other because all are from Adam and Eve, all have fallen short of the glory of God and therefore all are in need of salvation. Jesus has chosen love as the means for reconciling the nations to each other and to Himself.

Muslim evangelists didn't measure the intended quality of life for a Christian by studying the values of Jesus Christ. Instead, Muhammad and Muslim evangelists have been viewing the immoralities and temptations lived out by those bearing the name of "Christian." They have not discerned the work of the devil in the lives of these individuals and societies and have blamed their poor conduct on Christian values and teaching. They therefore present Christianity and the teachings of Christ as worthless and inferior to Islam, following the footsteps of Muhammad as reflected in the Qur'an:

O believers! of a truth, many of the teachers and monks[1] do devour man's substance in vanity, and turn them from the Way of God [Allah]. But to those who treasure up gold and silver and expend it not in the Way of God, announce tidings of a grievous torment (Q.9:34).

Incomplete Religions

Muslims hardly ever hear the Christian message because they have been informed that Islam is the best, last and most complete religion after Judaism and Christianity, and Muhammad is the last, true prophet of all:

Muhammad…is the Apostle of Allah, and the seal of the prophets (Q.33: 40).

He [Allah] it is who hath sent His Apostle with the Guidance and a religion of the truth, that He may make it victorious over every other religion, albeit they who assign partners[2] to God be averse from it (Q.9: 33).

The true religion with God is Islam (Q.3:19).

Therefore, according to the Qur'an, whatever the previous religions teach, they are incomplete in themselves.

Are these qur'anic claims based on knowledge, logical comparison and truth? Absolutely they are not. How could Muhammad be the seal of the prophets, who were assured of their future life, since Muhammad himself did not have such an assurance? How could Muhammad guide others with confidence if he himself was not sure about his own future? How could Islam be called the true and perfect religion since it was not able to release people from spiritual uncertainty in this life and unite them with God? Why would Christianity

---

1 Christian monks.

2 The Qur'an attributes the word "partners" to pagans who call idols the children of God, and to Christians who call Jesus the Son of God and consider him on the same level as God. The word "partner" or "associate" is considered as offensive and demeaning.

be called untrue, incomplete and imperfect since it was able to save people and establish them in the Kingdom of God from the life on earth?

The perfection of a faith is when the unity between God and mankind takes place practically and it is not left for the life after, as Islam does. The Gospel of Christ unites people with God in the life on earth.

If Muslims read the Qur'an in comparison with the Bible in the hands of Christians, they will be astonished at how Muhammad's claims were not based on knowledge and truth. Here are some superior stands of the Bible in comparison with the Qur'an:

- Allah is the creator of sin, but the God of the Bible is not. A god who creates sin cannot be a perfect role model for people and thereby cannot have a perfect messenger or religion.
- Muhammad is sinner, but Jesus is not. People need to follow the sinless One rather than a sinner. A sinner cannot guide people to righteousness. If Islam was a complete religion, it would give God's works to sinless Jesus to complete instead of giving them to sinful Muhammad.
- Jesus is alive and in heaven, but Muhammad died. Which one is the perfect living model for guiding people to life?

Muslims attribute the words "perfect" or "complete" or "true" to Islam, but none of them matches the imperfect and incomplete nature of Islam.

The Bible—Accurate or Altered?

The Qur'an states that Jesus and the prophets of the Old Testament foretold the coming of Muhammad:[1]

---

1 For further information read Ibn Hisham, *Sirat Raul Allah*, PP.203,204,206. & A. M. A. Shahrestani, *Tozih-almelal*, P.291 from book1.

> *Who shall follow the Apostle, the unlettered Prophet whom they shall find described with them in the Law and Evangel[1]...?* (Q.7:157).

> *And remember when Jesus the son of Mary said, "O children of Israel! of a truth I am God's apostle to you to confirm the law which was given before me, and to announce an apostle that shall come after me whose name shall be Ahmad!" But when he (Ahmad[2]) presented himself with clear proofs of his mission, they said, "This is manifest sorcery!"* (Q.61:6).

These statements do not exist in the Bible. For this reason, Muslims explain that the Bible lacks the prophecies about Muhammad, because its followers altered its verses.

Muslims need to realize that there are more documentary evidences for the reliability of the Bible than for any other book from the ancient world.[3] With the availability of these evidences it is impossible to build a case for where, when, how, and why the Bible was changed. There is no time, whether during the time of Muhammad or before or after him, in which Muslims can prove that any alteration in the Bible occurred. The Qur'an itself confirms and defends the Bible, as it existed in the seventh century, as the Word of God:

> *...it* [the Qur'an] *be the truth confirmatory of their* [Christians' and Jews'] *own Scriptures,...the confirmation of previous revelations* (Q.2:91, 97).

> *...believe in what* [the Qur'an] *we have sent down confirmatory of the Scripture in your* [Christians' and Jews'] *hands...* (Q.4:47).

> *And if thou* [Muhammad] *art in doubt as to what* [the Qur'an] *we have sent down to thee, inquire at those* [Christians and

---

1 Or "the Torah and the Gospel."
2 Equated by Muslims with Muhammad.
3 N.L. Geisler & A. Saleeh, PP.207-255. & North African Mission, *Reaching Muslims Today*, P.26.

Jews] *who have read the Scriptures before thee* (Q.10:94; c.f. Q.3:3; 5:46-48; 29:46; 6:92; 41:43).

These verses of the Qur'an reflect Muhammad's high view of biblical authority. He confirms the authority of the Bible and therefore commands Muslims to profess belief in the same Bible that his contemporary Jews and Christians were holding. Therefore, the Qur'an itself takes away any reason for the Muslim rejection of the authenticity of the Bible.

In fact, Muhammad himself doubted the Qur'an, needing to lean towards the Bible and to judge accordingly (Q.10:94-5). The following Hadith states that Muhammad liked to follow the People of Scriptures, Jews and Christians:

> *The Prophet used to copy the people of the Scriptures in matters in which there was no order from Allah. The people of the Scriptures used to let their hair hang down while the pagans used to part their hair. So the Prophet let his hair hang down first, but later on he parted it.*[1]

Although, there is not any Islamic evidence concerning the existence of the Bible in Arabic in Muhammad's time, but there is evidence for the existence of the Gospel:

> *A'isha, the wife of the Apostle of Allah (may peace be upon him), reported: The first (form) with which was started the revelation to the Messenger of Allah was the true vision in sleep. And he did not see any vision but it came like the bright gleam of dawn. Thenceforth solitude became dear to him and he used to seclude himself in the cave of Hira', where he would engage in tahannuth (and that is a worship for a number of nights) before returning to his family and getting provisions again for this purpose. He would then return to Khadija and take provisions for a like period, till Truth came upon him while he was in the cave of Hira'. There came to him the angel and said: Recite, to which he replied: I am not lettered. He took hold of me [the Apostle said] and pressed me, till I was*

---

1   Bukhari, V 7, B 72, H 799 & Bukhari, V 5, B 58, H 280.

hard pressed; thereafter he let me off and said: Recite. I said: I am not lettered. He then again took hold of me and pressed me for the second time till I was hard pressed and then let me off and said: Recite, to which I replied: I am not lettered. He took hold of me and pressed me for the third time, till I was hard pressed and then let me go and said: Recite in the name of your Lord Who created, created man from a clot of blood. Recite. And your most bountiful Lord is He Who taught the use of pen, taught man what he knew not (al-Qur'an, xcvi. 1-4). Then the Prophet returned therewith, his heart was trembling, and he went to Khadija and said: Wrap me up, wrap me up! So they wrapped him till the fear had left him. He then said to Khadija: O Khadija! what has happened to me? and he informed her of the happening, saying: I fear for myself. She replied: It can't be. Be happy. I swear by Allah that He shall never humiliate you. By Allah, you join ties of relationship, you speak the truth, you bear people's burden, you help the destitute, you entertain guests, and you help against the vicissitudes which affect people. Khadija then took him to **Waraqa b. Naufal** *b. Asad b. 'Abd al-'Uzza, and he was the son of Khadija's uncle, i. e., the brother of her father. And he was the man who had embraced Christianity in the Days of Ignorance (i. e. before Islam) and he* **used to write books in Arabic and, therefore, wrote Injil in Arabic as God willed that he should write.** *He was very old and had become blind Khadija said to him: O uncle! listen to the son of your brother. Waraqa b. Naufal said: O my nephew! what did you see? The Messenger of Allah (may peace be upon him), then, informed him what he had seen, and Waraqa said to him: It is namus that God sent down to Musa. Would that I were then (during your prophetic career) a young man. Would that I might be alive when your people would expel you! The Messenger of Allah (may peace be upon him) said: Will they drive me out? Waraqa said: Yes. Never came a man with a like* *of what you have brought but met hostilities. If I see your day I shall help you wholeheartedly.*[1] [Bold added.]

Muhammad had confidence in his cousin Nofel (Naufal) and through him had built his trust in the current Bible and confirmed its authenticity. Since the age of 12, Muhammad attended the churches in Mecca and in Damascus (anytime he accompanied his uncle Abutalib with his caravan to Damascus) up until the age of 52 when he still was in Mecca. He must have heard many good things about the Bible. However, after migrating to Medina, his life was not pleasing to Christians and Jews. He chose a different path to his early Meecan life when he was in contact with Christians. In Medina, he adapted himself to the practices of his newly befriended tribe and got involved with looting Meccan caravans and terrorizing his oppositions.

Medina had never experiences such a blood-shed which Muhammad made for his follower habitual progressively. After fleeing from Mecca to Medina as a refugee, he portrayed himself as a peaceful man and prophet. The democratic atmosphere of Medina was like a safe haven for him to say or believe in anything he wanted. He only got oppositions later when he was involved in caravan looting. His unethical actions shocked the inhabitants of Medina on how a peaceful prophet of a peaceful religion sanctioned the invasion of caravans, looting others and killing those who cared for their communities. Some highly respected people, who worried about the insecurity Muhammad was creating in their homeland, criticized him for his strange teaching and actions. In response, he sent his people at nights and killed them secretly. We can understand from Muhammad's own biography, *The Life of Muhammad*, on how a peaceful Muhammad changed into someone who never tolerated critiques and opposition. An elderly man named Abu Afak expressed his dissatisfaction of Muhammad's actions through a poem, asking his hosting tribe to withdraw from the leadership of the prophet of Islam and follow someone else:

---

1   Muslim, B 1, H 301.

> *Long have I lived but never have I seen*
> *An assembly or collection of people*
> *More faithful to their undertaking*
> *And their allies when called upon*
> *Than the sons of Qayla when they assembled,*
> *Men who overthrew mountains and never submitted,*
> *A rider who came to them split them in two (saying)*
> *"Permitted", "Forbidden", of all sorts of things.*
> *Had you believed in glory or kingship*
> *You would have followed Tubba.*[1]

Muhammad, unable to bear this criticism, sent his devoted followers at night and they stabbed him to death at his bed. This hostile attitude towards an elderly man outraged the inhabitants of Medina, and as a result, a woman named Asma requested retaliation, as the law of the land necessitated. She wrote:

> *I despise B. Malik and al-Nabit*
> *and Auf and B. al-Khazraj.*
> *You obey a stranger who is none of yours,*
> *One not of Murad or Madhhij.*
> *Do you expect good from him after the killing of your chiefs*
> *Like a hungry man waiting for a cook's broth?*
> *Is there no man of pride who would attack him by surprise*
> *And cut off the hopes of those who expect aught from him?*[2]

Muhammad sent his messengers at night again and they slaughtered her in front of her very young children.[3] Since then, the denial of the prophet-hood of Muhammad was seen as an offense in Islam and its judiciary system; the common method sanctioned by Muhammad is beheading.

This not only took him away from his previous Christian practices and beliefs but also turned him to be an accuser of

---

1 Inb Ishaq, P. 675.

2 Ibid, PP. 675-6.

3 Ibid, P. 676.

Christianity and the Bible which condemn any invasion of freedom and rights of others. He and the heads of his hosting tribe were well aware that the only way to turn people's eyes from their own wrong actions was to accuse others and make people busy with blaming others. This was what he also did to Christians. He first expressed his opposition to the Bible in a Gnostic way, the already established tool for accusing Christians. He might have heard these unfair Gnostic criticisms via the preaching in the church in Mecca. However, after conquering the whole Arabian Peninsula, he rejected all beliefs that were linked to the Bible, including Gnosticism, and said: *I will expel the Jews and Christians from the Arabian Peninsula and will not leave any but Muslim.*[1] It was after this that he openly called the Bible a *concealed* book:

> *Desire ye then that for your sakes the Jews should believe? Yet a part of them heard the word of God, and then, after they had understood it, perverted it, and knew that they did so* (Q.2:75).

> *…the Book which Moses brought, a light and guidance to man, which ye set down on paper, publishing part, but concealing most* (Q.6:91; c.f. Q.2:146, 159, 174; 4: 46; 5:13-15, 41).

More than a century after Muhammad's death, Muslim apologists broadened the accusation, adding one extra thing, *the omission of Muhammad's name in the Bible.* They searched the entire Bible and were unable to find Muhammad's name in it. Of course, they were not able to even think that Muhammad could have been wrong since speaking beyond the words of Muhammad was equal to death, the easy and safer conclusion was to blame Christians and Jews and say that they removed the name of Muhammad from the Bible and corrupted it.

The pressure of Islam has always prevented Muslims of comparing the existing inconsistencies between the Qur'an and the Bible logically and theologically and kept them ignorant of

---

1 Muslim :: Book 19 : Hadith 4366 & Read Q.3:19; 9:33.

the real reason for the disunity among these two books. As a result, the baseless rejection of the Bible became a custom for Muslims ever since the rise of Islam as a political religion. Because of this, diving into the depths of the world of reasoned thinking and research in Islamic societies has always been costly. Some Muslims who have done this have been excluded from their social rights and even sentenced to death. For this reason many dare not to study the facts and the evidence in order to avoid mistreatment by Islamic authorities or even their own followers. They therefore prefer to follow in the traditional footsteps.

For Muslim scholars, the validity of the Bible is surprisingly not based on whether the book provides salvation; rather it is based on whether the book contains the name of Muhammad. How many Muslim scholars have shown any interest in discovering whether the Qur'an or the Bible best meets the immediate need of humankind for salvation? All they have done is to explain the difference between the Qur'an and the Bible according to the doctrine of corruption and alteration of the written text.[1] Their goal is to discourage Muslims from reading the Bible.

It is time for Muslim leaders and scholars to help their followers and readers understand that the real difference between these books is the salvation which is provided by the Bible, not not by the Qur'an. This is more productive than concentrating on issues which have nothing to do with eternal destiny. What people need to discover is how they can be united with their Creator immediately, and which book prepares the ground for this unity. Wise leadership is one that bases its motives on people's real needs and leads them to meet their needs through personal experience.

A Christian man who was from an Islamic background answered a Muslim lady's comment about the Bible having been altered. He said, "The Bible that you think has been changed, has changed the status of my life from the dominion of darkness to

---

1 One example is Bukhari :: Book 3 :: Volume 48 :: Hadith 850

the kingdom of heaven." What really mattered for that person was that the words of the Bible have a saving power that saved his life, no matter what other people thought or said about it.

Curiously, Muslim scholars still give credence to some of what the Bible says. While on the one hand Muslim scholars disclaim the authenticity of the Bible, on the other hand they are prepared to take its scriptures and interpret the verses to support their own claims about the prophetic ministry of Muhammad.[1]

The vital thing that makes the Bible different from the Qur'an is not the absence of Muhammad's name in the Bible, but the assurance of salvation that it contains. The Bible testifies to the salvation that God has provided through His Son, Jesus Christ. No such assurance of salvation is to be found in the Qur'an.

My initial interest in the Bible was not because of the name of Jesus Christ or the fact that He was called God's Son. Such ideas were actually obstacles to me because of my irrational Islamic approach to the Bible. However, it was my certain need of salvation that drew my attention to the pages of the Bible. For me to meet God and gain eternal life was the most important thing. This unavoidable need for eternal life led me to put everything else at a lower priority than my salvation. I therefore sought to approach the words of the Bible in its truest sense:

> *Your covenant with death will be annulled, And your agreement with Sheol will not stand* (Isa. 28:18).

> *…my eyes have seen Your salvation, Which you have prepared before the face all peoples, A light to bring revelation to the Gentiles, And the glory of Your people Israel* (Luke 2:30-32).

> *"God has visited His people." And this report about Him went throughout all Judea and the surrounding region* (Luke 7:16-17).

---

1 Read N.L. Geisler & A. Saleeh, PP.147-154.

> *For God so loved the world that He gave His only begotten Son, that whoever believes in Him should not perish but have everlasting life* (John 3:16).

> *I [Jesus] say to you, he who hears My words and believes in Him who sent Me has everlasting life, and shall not come into judgment, he has passed from death into life* (John 5:24).

My spiritual needs led me to test the words of the Bible against all the dimensions of my life. Wonderfully my needs were met by the words of the Bible that acted as the power of God unto my salvation. Therefore, because of this awe-inspiring experience, my soul united with the life giving Spirit of the Bible who is called Jesus, the One who is God, or the Son of God.

What is amazing about the Bible and has made it more reliable and trustworthy than any other book in the world, is the unity of its message on how God will come and carry on the work of salvation. Forty people wrote the whole Bible over about 1,600 years. The passing of these many years could not erase the vital message of God from the pages of the Bible. Neither political conditions nor economic and social situations could create disharmony among the 40 writers of the Bible even over such a long period of time.

The message of the Bible is plain. It says that no one except the Almighty God could save people from their sins. Therefore, everyone, including the prophets, relied on the saving act of the coming God (the Son), and taught others this truth. Even the sins of the prophets were not a threat to the uniqueness of this message. The prophets and the great kings could not twist the promise of God in order to excuse their sins, because they had understood and believed the truth of the message. The only solution they found for their sins was to confess them, regardless of the office they held (c.f. Psalms 51; Isaiah 6:1-5).

The book of Genesis in the Bible states that Christ, the Son, will come and destroy the work of Satan. This unchangeable promise of God became the faith of every writer of the Bible from the beginning to the end (Genesis 3:15; 1 John 3:8). Therefore, by the Spirit of God all the writers of the Bible pointed people to the coming of the Son, Jesus Christ, who came with the full glory of God to save and unite people:

> *For it pleased the Father that in Him all the fullness should dwell, and by Him to reconcile all things to Himself, by Him, whether things on earth or things in heaven, having made peace through the blood of His cross* (Colossians 1:19-20).

The revelation of God's full glory in Jesus Christ is the central message in the Bible that united the forty writers of the Bible over such a long period of time.

The Qur'an—Complete Revelation from God?

Islam's own evidences—as they were mentioned earlier—prove that there are verses in the Qur'an which are not from Allah but merely from Muhammad and his companions. This contradicts the words of the Qur'an, which presents the idea that if the Qur'an were from any other source than God, it would have been full of contradictions:

> *Can they not consider the Koran? Were it from any other than God, they would surely have found in it many contradictions* (Q.4:82).

Contradictions!? The Quran is full of contradictions. We learn from Islamic traditions that the present Qur'an was rejected or judged as incomplete by some of Muhammad's followers, including his fourth successor and son-in-law, Ali.[1] His

---

1 Salim Ibn-Ghaisse (Death 90 H.G., 80 years after the death of Muhammad) writes in his book, "It was the time of Uthman's caliphate that in a meeting Ali talked boldly and answered people's questions from morning to midday. He reminded the audience of what Muhammad said, 'Ali's relation to me is like Aaron's to Moses.' As part of the conversation, Ali confirmed that the Qur'an

rejection was mainly due to contradictions in this version of the Qur'an arising from a standardization attempt carried out by Uthman, the third successor after Muhammad's death. The vulnerability of the Qur'an, due to alteration of the text or replacement of certain texts, in turn, brought about divisions among Muslim leaders. This fueled disunity among them after Muhammad's death, even to the point of bitter rivalry or war.[1]

Uthman ordered the destruction of all the other Qur'ans in circulation and presented the current text as the true standard. Islam's own theological and historical background proves that the present Qur'an cannot be regarded as perfect, and this is made very clear when one considers the many differences that existed among the various qur'anic texts:[2]

- Time and time we read in the Islamic traditions that some qur'anic verses were missing and the leaders needed the counsel and witness of various people and writers over the authenticity of those verses.[3] The Qur'an that has been standardized as correct is one which a *man* (not God), according to his *own choice* and not by revelation, decreed to be the true one.

---

he collected was the most authentic and complete one. Parts of the present Qur'an were eaten by a sheep and many verses of the Suras (Chapters) 24, 33 and 49 were also missing." [For further information read Salim Ibn-Ghaisse, *Asrar Aal Muhammad (The Mysteries of Muhammad's Descendants),* Iran-Ghom: Translated by B. Alef, 1980. (1400 Hijri-Ghamari), PP.70-73,82-3.]

1 While Muhammad was alive he realised that alterations of the Qur'an were causing divisions among his followers and he taught strongly in the Qur'an that any division would discredit the mission of Islam (Q.6:159).

2 Read J. Gilchrist, *The Textual History of the Qur'an and the Bible,* PP.15-21. & Salim Ibn-Ghaisse, *Asrar Aal Muhammad,* PP.82-85.

3 Bukhari :: 9 :: Volume 89 :: Hadith 301. & Bukhari :: Volume 4 :: Book 52 :: Hadith 62.

- The theology of Islam speaks of one unchangeable heavenly text, whereas the followers of Muhammad had a variety of versions of the Qur'an.
- The evidence proves that the codex of Ibn Mas'ud was singled out by Muhammad as the best Qur'an available; however, this is not the basis for the present text.[1]
- There is evidence that, to this day, verses and, indeed, whole passages are still omitted from the Qur'an.[2]
- The Qura'an itself states that people made it into shreds (Q.15:90-91).
- Many Muslim jurists confirm the alteration of the Qur'an.[3]

Therefore, no one can honestly claim that the Qur'an, in itself, has the authority of being God's eternal speech and His full revelation since it was not immune to changes.[4] If it were God's full revelation, there would be no evidence of its being changed in any significant way. Clearly, this is not the case.

Three Gods?

The Qur'an claims that Christians have false beliefs about God. It says that Christians believe in three gods:

> *Infidels now are they who say, "God is the Messiah, Son of Mary."... They surely are infidels who say, "God is the third of three": for there is no God but one God: and if they refrain not from what they say, a grievous chastisement shall light on such of them as are infidels* (Q.5:72-73).

On one hand, the trinity that the Qur'an mentions is something quite different from the one that exists in the Bible and

---

1 Muslim :: Book 31 : Hadith 6024. & Bukhari :: Volume 5 :: Book 58 :: Hadith 150.

2 Ibn Ishaq, Sirat Rasulullah, P.684.

3 John Burton, *The Encyclopedia of Islam*, vol. 7, s.v. "Naskh," P. 1010.

4 K. Cragg, *The Call of the Minaret*, New York: Oxford University Press, 1956, P.54.

Christian faith. The Qur'an records that Christians worship *three* gods—*God, Mary* and *Jesus*:

> *O ye people of the Book!... say not, "Three"* (Q.4:171).

> *And when God shall say—"O Jesus, Son of Mary: hast thou said unto mankind—'Take me and my mother as two Gods, beside God'?"* (Q.5:116).

This has led Muslims to believe that Christians are blasphemous and believe in various gods. Muslims, on the other hand, interpret the word "Son" in a physical sense contrary to its real meaning in the Gospel. They say that God is spirit and therefore He could not have had a physical relationship with Mary, producing a son like Jesus. Jesus is only a created man who was a prophet.

It is sad that for centuries Muslims have been rejecting Christians due to fallacious teaching. The Bible does not present Mary as a God, and Jesus' birth as the result of a physical relationship between God and Mary. In the Bible God is one, and has revealed Himself in three personalities, the Father, the Son and the Holy Spirit. With the coming of the Spirit upon the Virgin Mary, the Spirit became flesh (Jesus the Son) and revealed Himself fully. In the Bible, the understanding of the Trinity is something that leads the person to the only one and true God. This is the most gracious opportunity that the unique God has provided for all humankind, by becoming man, dwelling with us and relating Himself to us through His personalities. The Qur'an itself records this spiritual event (the coming of Jesus into the world) exactly as it is in the Bible:

> *Remember when the angel said, "O Mary! Verily God announceth to thee the Word from Him: His name shall be, Messiah Jesus the son of Mary, illustrious in this world, and in the next, and one of those who have near access to God.... She said, "How, O my Lord! shall I have a son, when man hath not touched me?" He said, "Thus: God will create what*

He will; When He decreeth a thing, He only saith, 'Be,' and it is" (Q.3:45, 47).

Other texts from the Qur'an refer to Jesus being born as a man, but not the result of a physical relationship between God and Mary.

The Messiah, Jesus, son of Mary, is only an apostle of God, and his Word which he conveyed into Mary, and a Spirit proceeding from him (Q.4.171).

…we [God] sent our spirit to her [Mary], and he [Jesus] took before her the form of a perfect man (Q.19:17).

Unfortunately Muslims are not aware that these verses of the Qur'an mean that God became man (Jesus) and dwelt among His creatures.

The above verses carry the meaning that the "Spirit of God" and the "Word of God" became *Jesus*. God is Word and Spirit. The One and only God revealed Himself in Jesus. It is the same as the Bible, which proclaims that the Word "God" or the Spirit "God" became Jesus.

The following verses from the Bible support the Christian teaching of the Trinity.

…the angel said to her, "Do not be afraid, Mary, you have found favor with God… The Holy Spirit will come upon you, and the power of the Highest will overshadow you; therefore, also that Holy One who is to be born will be called the Son of God" (Luke 1:30, 35).

In the beginning was the Word, and the Word was with God, and the Word was God. He was in the beginning with God. All things were made through Him, and without Him nothing was made that was made…. And the Word became flesh and dwelt among us, and we beheld His glory, the glory as of the only begotten of the Father, full of grace and truth (John 1:1-3, 14).

These verses, whether from the Qur'an (see previous page) or from the Bible, speak of the Trinity. God sent His Spirit and the Spirit became Jesus (the Son). Introducing the Triune characteristics of God in the Bible has nothing to do with the matter of "three gods." In the Bible, the One and only God introduces Himself as the *Father*, the *Son* and the *Holy Spirit*. These three persons of the One God are one in nature and inseparable to one another and are united in God's eternal unity. Therefore, the three personalities of the One God cannot be treated as three separate gods.

Some Islamic commentators maintain that the spirit in the above qur'anic verses (Q.4:171; 19:17) is not the Spirit of God, but the spirit of the Archangel. This idea hardly fits with the theology of Islam. If the Qur'an does not accept that the Spirit of God became man, then it will also be hard to accept that the spirit of an angel, which is the angel himself, became man. According to the Qur'an, giving Jesus the title of God is "the overstepping of Christians beyond their religious bounds" (Q.4:171). Giving Jesus the title of Archangel must also be seen in the same way.

We can understand from both the Bible and the Qur'an that the Spirit that came upon Mary was from God and was God. The essence of such a belief reveals a great theological fact which extends beyond the imagination of Muslims. The Bible says, *"The one who comes from above is above all; the one who is from the earth belongs to the earth, and speaks as one from the earth. The one who comes from heaven is above all. He testifies to what he has seen and heard"* (John 3:31-34). The Spirit that has come from above is revealed as a person who is above Adam and his descendants. Secondly, He is the Spirit that is from God (and was and will be with God), who became flesh and dwelt among humankind and who ascended back to heaven from where He came. The Spirit has always identified Himself with God and Jesus. He is the spokesman of either Jesus or God, and this implies the interrelationship between Jesus and God.

His prime reason for coming to earth is to be a man who reveals all that heaven has undertaken to save humankind. This teaching is not foreign to the verses of the Qur'an that talk about Jesus. The similarity arises from the fact that the Qur'an has borrowed the exact events from the Bible. In similar fashion to the Bible, the Qur'an also states that Jesus is the Word and Spirit of God who came down from heaven, became flesh, did the job for which He was sent and ascended back to heaven again. There is therefore an exact revelation of the Trinity when the Qur'an mentions the words, "God," "Spirit" (or "Word") and "Jesus."

The Trinity is not three gods. It is the three persons of the One God revealed as part of the plan of salvation to redeem us in all the dimensions of human life. God is one in His nature and essence, but His essence reveals His personalities to save sinful humankind according to His love, justice and holiness. God didn't have to reveal His persons. It was because of our needs that He stretched Himself towards us. God's work is not isolated from our needs in daily life. God is the loving God. What He desires is to have us back home. God is also holy and just. The triune personalities of God all work together simultaneously to open the eyes of people to accepting the saving acts of God.

When we invite God into our lives, and let His Spirit and Word and Love express His Oneness to us, only then will we be able to understand that the Trinity of the Bible is something that stands for One God, not three. When Christians say that God is One, it is not simply a statement, but God's witness to the Truth through His Spirit. And His ministry can only be experienced by Christians through their faith in Christ. It is the blessing of the three personalities of One God that has enabled Christians to meet God in Jesus Christ, the Son, and to call Him Emmanuel, which means "God with us" (Matthew 1:23), not "*gods* with us."

The idea of three gods asserted by Muslim evangelists reflects their great misunderstanding of the Christian faith. This obstacle can be removed from the minds of Muslim evangelists only when they get the courage to read the words of the Bible in depth and so discover God's plan for salvation. They need to understand and to discover the central theme of the Bible, which is found through the authority of the Son's name, Jesus Christ.

Teachers Equal with God?

The Qur'an accuses Jews and Christians of claiming that their teachers and priests are equal to God:

> *They* [Jews and Christians] *take their teachers, and their monks,…as Lords beside God, though bidden to worship one God only. There is no God but He! Far from His glory be what they associate with Him* (Q.9:31).

This assertion is foreign to the teaching of the Bible. The very convincing, simple and understandable message of the Bible is the uniqueness of God. Even every Jewish and Christian child knows that the whole story of creation, the stories of Noah, Abraham and the exodus from Egypt were the work of none other than the One and only living God.

There were ample worldly opportunities for the disciples of Jesus Christ, supported by their great miracles, to claim themselves as gods, but it was impossible for them, because they had understood that there was no god besides God. When the apostles Paul and Barnabas heard that people called them gods because of the miracle that Paul carried out, they both tore their clothes and rushed out into the crowd, shouting

> *Men, why are doing these things? We also are men with the same nature as you, and preach to you that you should turn from these useless things to the living God* (Acts 14:15).

It is very hard to believe that Jews called their teachers "lords" with the same status as God, when the main reason that Jews rejected Christians and started persecuting them was because they called Jesus God. There has never been a friendly acceptance of Christians by fundamentalist Jews because of Christianity's belief in the deity of Christ. Jews accused Christians of claiming a man (Jesus) as equal to God. How then could they come to call their teachers deities?

The message of the Bible is based on the uniqueness of God from the beginning to the end. The Bible says that God is one and there is no one like Him.

Here are some examples from the Old Testament:

Who is like You, O LORD, among the gods? Who is like You, glorious in holiness, Fearful in praises, doing wonders? (Exodus 15:11).

All my bones shall say, "LORD, who is like You, Delivering the poor from him who is too strong for him, Yes, the poor and needy from him who plunders him (Psalms 35:10).

Your righteousness, O God, is very high, You who have done great things: O God, who is like You? (Psalms 71:19).

Now from the New Testament:

There is one God, and there is not other but He (Mark 12:32).

...there is one God ... (Romans 3:30).

So, it is obvious that there is no substance to the assertion by Muslim evangelists that Christian and Jewish teachers are believed to be equal with God. There is no support for it in the teaching of Christianity and Judaism. Rather, Islam has distorted the truth to bring condemnation by its adherents against Christians and Jews.

Teaching on Acceptance or Religious Discrimination

So Much Sorrow for the Sons and Daughters of Adam and Eve

The misinformation spread by Muhammad and Muslim evangelists was mixed with religious and political prejudices resulted in the total disqualification of Christians and Jews:

Non-Muslims are unclean (najis in Arabic) (Q.9:28).

For the worst of beasts are those who reject Allah and will not believe in him. (Q.8:55).

Muslims were misled and told that they had to avoid any positive relationship with Christians and Jews, because they are from unclean nations. Christians and Jews can be regarded as clean only when they become Muslims. Therefore, any Muslim who touches a Christian or a Jew must be ceremonially washed.[1] This is the most upsetting of behaviors to be practiced by the fanatical children of Adam and Eve against their other brothers and sisters from the same root and substance. This must cause so much sorrow and embarrassment for Adam and Eve as parents, and must be an unbearable attitude in God's eyes, the one who has created all humankind from the same substance. This religious discrimination is also a dishonor to the world and cannot match with the message of peace among nations. Every person who is familiar with the words of Christ will understand that the theology of Islam has completely distanced itself from the loving Spirit of Christ whose task is to embrace everyone, Jews and Gentiles, equally (Ephesians 1:9-10; Galatians 3:28; 2 Corinthians 3:17).

---

1 R. Khomeini, *Tozih Almasael,* Iran-Mashhad: Baresh Pub., 2000 (1379 Hijra), P.32,526. & A. Khamaneie, *Ajubatol-esteftaat* (in Dari Farsi), Tehran: Saghalain Pub., 1997 (1376 Hijra), P.92.

In the Absence of the Gospel

Muslim evangelists often accuse the Christian religion of being unable to discipline its followers for their immorality. In saying this they do not examine the Christian faith through the words of Jesus Christ, but through the behavior of those who claim to be Christians. Whenever they see immorality in any part of the Christian world, they see it as a defect of real Christian faith. They ignore and do not read about what the Gospel of Jesus Christ says about morality or immorality. This ignorance is because they think the Gospel is corrupted and hence they make no effort to discover the basis for Christian moral values in the Gospel. As a result, they have unfortunately judged the Christian faith in the absence of an understanding of the Gospel. They only look at the immorality of the Christian world, which is also alien to the faith of the Gospel of Jesus Christ, and use this as a basis for their criticism and rejection of the Christian faith. They believe that the immorality in the Christian world results from the incompleteness of the Christian religion. This is a great theological mistake when someone criticizes a religion for the immoralities of its nominal followers without considering whether or not the religion itself is the cause of those immoralities. In a similar way, it would be wrong for someone to come and criticize Islam on the basis of the wrongdoing of Muslims, unless Islam presents itself to be the cause of that wrongdoing. For this reason, Muslims first need to discover whether the Gospel in the hands of Christians encourages the Christian world towards immorality or not. It is after this investigation that they will be able to realize the real cause of immorality in so-called Christian societies.

It is worth it to say that Muslim scholars sometimes blame others for some immoralities that are called moral in Islam if they are performed under the Islamic instructions. For example, it is called adultery if a man and woman establish any romantic relationship with each other outside marriage. But, if the man is a Muslim, he can marry her in the presence of a religious Muslims leader in exchange for food or money for a day or a week or longer or shorter. This is called a legitimate short-term marriage in Islam. This marriage will automatically be terminated at the end of the fixed time or date. This is what Muhammad and his contemporary followers put into practice[1] and is still in practice among some Islamic communities.

There is another shocking decree by Muhammad concerning a Muslim male and female who are not married to one another but work together in a room when there are no others. It is unlawful for them to be in a room unless the female has suckled the male. After doing so, he becomes her foster child and they can be with each other without any problem.[2]

Isn't it shocking when the performers of these immoral actions forget to see their own immoralities but easily blame others for the same things!

---

1 Muslim :: Book 8 : Hadith 3258. & Bukhari :: Volume 6 :: Book 60 :: Hadith 139.
2 Muslim :: Book 8 : Hadith 3426.

4

Ambiguities in the Teaching of Muhammad

Politics or Theology?

Tolerance or War?

Forgiveness of Sin and Salvation

The Son of God?

Teaching on the Crucifixion

Teaching on Morality

Politics or Theology?

Many verses of the Qur'an and the traditional statements of Muhammad reveal the fact that Muhammad's decisions to write or revise the qur'anic texts were subject to his or his companions' unstable political trends. He substituted Allah's verses in some parts of the Qur'an with his own words or those of his companions in order to justify his actions. This instability meant that any idea that Muhammad accepted at one time could be rejected at another. Even the fundamental beliefs of his ministry would change according to the current situation. For example, while he was under pressure by the Meccan pagans early in his ministry because of his opposition to paganism, he recited verses in praise of idols in order to win the favor of some powerful pagan leaders and gain momentum. Another example was when he changed the prayer direction from Jerusalem to Mecca. Before capturing Mecca, Muhammad had told Muslim that Allah had decreed them to pray five times a day toward Jerusalem, the dwelling place of the true God. He changed the prayer direction after migrating to Medina. Jews did not follow him and he became angry at them and did not want to pray toward Jerusalem, a Jewish city, anymore. He ordered Muslims to pray towards Ka'bah, the pagan shrine in Mecca, and said to them that Allah changed his mind:

> *The change is a difficulty, but not to those whom Allah has guided.... we will have thee turn thy face to kebla the sacred Mosque[1].... Even though thou shouldest bring every kind of sign to those who have received the Scriptures [Jews], yet thy kebla[2] they will not adopt; nor shalt thou adopt their kebla* (Q.2:143-145)

These verses clearly state that the Muslims' previous Kebla (prayer direction) was Jerusalem, which belonged to the Jews.

---

1 The house of worship in Mecca, called "Ka'bah" which is equal to Temple.

2 Kebla means "prayer direction" to Mecca from wherever Muslims live.

Allah had ordained in eternity (as the Qur'an is thought to be pre-existent) that Muhammad and his Muslim followers had to pray toward Jerusalem. Then thousands years later, Allah became angry at the Jews for not following Muhammad and therefore changed his eternal decision and showed Muslims a different direction, which was rejected in eternity as a place of idols! What a capricious god!?

On the other hand, the Qur'an states that the house of worship (Ka'bah) in Mecca was made the holiest place of worship by Allah. Allah commanded both Abraham and his son Ishmael to build it for his (yet coming) Muslims so that they could pray toward it. The Qur'an states that after the completion of the Ka'bah, Abraham prayed to Allah asking him to make his posterity the true Muslims and to raise a prophet among them to honor the rites and rituals of the religion of Abraham:

> *The first temple that was founded for mankind, was that in Becca[1] In it are evident signs, even the standing-place of Abraham: and he who entereth it is safe. And the pilgrimage to the temple, is a service due to God from those who are able to journey thither* (Q.3:96-97; also 2:125-129).

If these verses of the Qur'an were true, why did Allah (in reality Muhammad) choose Jerusalem for prayer direction first instead of Mecca? Wouldn't it be easier for people to learn the truth and devote themselves to it from the beginning rather than being confused?

The initial rejection of Mecca and the acceptance of Jerusalem can only be understood in the light of two things: 1) his friendship with contemporary Christians in Mecca and 2), his interest in the widespread Jewish way of life which superseded the nomadic way of life. He changed his mind in Medina because Christians and Jews were no longer friends to him.

---

1 Place of crowding, i.e. Mecca.

The Islamic tradition states Muhammad's *disinterest* as the definite reason for changing the prayer direction.[1] Traditions say that Muhammad's companions, who were Arabs from Medina, did not have a good history of relationships with the Jews even before the rise of Islam. The first non-Jewish habitants of Medina who went to Mecca and accepted Muhammad's call were a group of six from the tribe of *Khazraj* who were the sworn enemies to the Jews in Medina. *Khazrajites* were pagan worshippers and were not befriended by the Jews. Jews continually threatened them by telling them about the coming of the future prophet (the Messiah who was foretold in the Old Testament) who would end every blasphemy.[2] Thinking that Muhammad was this Messiah, the Khazrajites made haste to gain the favor of Muhammad before the Jews. Therefore, they went to Mecca from Medina, made a mutual treaty with Muhammad and joined his movement. The treaty included vows made against the Jewish tribes in Medina. The Khazrajites vowed to welcome Muhammad into Medina and treat him as a member of their tribe. In return, Muhammad vowed to fight their enemies along with them and to make peace with anyone the Khazrajites called friends.

It was after this union that Muhammad's disenchantment with the Jews evolved.[3] He legitimized war against non-Muslims and encouraged all Muslims to gather together in order to increase their strength so that a religious war could be enforced.[4] This of course angered the Jews because Muhammad was not a Jew but an Ishmaelite and therefore, he could not be the promised prophet. Also, Muhammad had made a vow with the Khazrajites to get rid of the Jews. The Jews felt threatened and began to strengthen their already existing relationship (more economic)

---

1 Tabari, Muhammad-bin Jarir, *Tarikh-al-rosol val-molouk,* PP.941-2.

2 Ibn Hisham, *Sirat Rasul Allah,* P.198.

3 Ibid, PP.203-4.

4 Tabari, Muhammad-bin Jarir, *Tarikh-al-rosol val-molouk,* PP.894-6,902-3,907-8. & Ibn Hisham, *Sirat Rasul Allah,* PP.204-5.

against the threats of Muhammad's unity with Khazrajites. This fueled Muhammad's determination in fulfilling his promise to Khazrajites. He launched various attacks on the Jews, resulting in expelling them or their annihilation. The Qur'an calls his attitudes to the Jews as heavenly:

> *And those of the People of the Book who aided them – Allah did take them down from their strongholds and cast terror into their hearts. (So that) some ye slew, and some ye made prisoners* (Q.33:26).

Another reason for the rejection of the Jews could have been related to their treatment of Salman Farsi, who was a slave placed in the hands of a Jew in Medina. As already mentioned in Section 1, Salman was heading toward Mecca in order to visit Muhammad. Meccan caravan travelers sold him to a Jew. Salman had more than likely informed Muhammad of this. After his immigration to Medina, Muhammad bought Salman and released him. Salman grew in his friendship with Muhammad and became one of the powerful figures in Islamic army.[1] Therefore, this and other similar events fueled Muhammad's growing anger toward the Jews.

Christian communities also felt threatened after Muhammad started to criticize Christianity. Therefore, Christian communities sent their leaders to Muhammad in order to stop any future tension or attacks. Even though, their intention was to solve the problem peacefully, but Muhammad rejected their beliefs and placed before them two rigid options: to become Muslims or to pay tribute (*jizya*, a payment extorted to secure life).[2] It was after this that he started to deny the sonship of Jesus Christ, His divinity and the Trinity. Whereas previously, he had stated that Christians were above all others and their future was bright:

---

1 Ibn Hisham, *Sirat Rasul Allah,* P.98.
2 Ibn Hisham, *Sirat Rasul Allah,* PP.188-9,491-516, 643.

God said,…I will place those who follow thee [Jesus] *above those who believe not, until the day of resurrection* (Q.3:55).

Verily, they who believe [Muslims]*, and they who follow the Jewish religion, and the Christians, and the Sabeites--whoever of these believeth in God and the last day, and doeth which is right, shall have their reward with their Lord: fear shall not come upon them, neither shall they be grieved* (Q.2:62).

However, he later announced his most heartbreaking and shocking decree, saying:

Kill those who join other gods with God wherever ye shall find them: and seize them, besiege them, and lay wait for them with every kind of ambush: but if they shall convert, and observe prayer, and pay the obligatory alms, then let them go their way, for God is gracious, Merciful (Q.9:5).

Muhammad's wavering political stance toward other nations and religions influenced Islam more than theological fact. History and the Qur'an record the results of his instability which laid the groundwork for this major world religion.

Tolerance or War?

Muhammad's thinking moved toward heretical opinions about Jesus and he started accusing Christians of misinterpreting the Bible. Even so, he still expected Christians to stay supportive of him despite all the changes. However, they refused to welcome him anymore. That caused him to become angry and to change his friendly stance toward Christians to one of confrontation:

O believers! take not the Jews or Christians as friends. They are but one another's friends. If any one of you taketh them for his friends, he surely is one of them! God will not guide the evil doers (Q.5:51).

Whoso desireth any other religion than Islam, that religion shall never be accepted from him, and in the next world he shall be among the lost (Q.3:85).

According to the words of Muhammad, those who do not believe in Islam must be severely punished in this world and no one should be able to support them:

> *And as to those who believe not, I will chastise them with a terrible chastisement in this world and in the next; and none shall they have to help them* (Q.3:56).

This is a complete contradiction to the words of Jesus:

> *"But I say to you, love your enemies, bless those who curse you, do good to those who hate you, and pray for those who spitefully use you and persecute you, "that you be sons of your Father in heaven; for He makes His sun rise on the evil and on the good, and sends rain on the just and on the unjust* (Matthew 5:44-45).

Through the leadership of Jesus Christ, Christians see God as the source of "love" for all humankind regardless of their race, beliefs and nationalities. God proved His love through His revelation and atoning work in the Son, Jesus Christ. God did this in order to attract, save and return the lost to the state that existed before the fall. The Gospel of the Son teaches us:

> *[L]ove is of God; and everyone who loves is born of God and knows God. He who does not love does not know God, for God is love. In this the love of God was manifested toward us, that God has sent His only begotten Son into the world, that we might live through Him. In this is love, not that we loved God, but that He loved us and sent His Son to be the propitiation for our sins. Beloved, if God so loved us, we also ought to love one another. No one has seen God at any time. If we love one another, God abides in us, and His love has been perfected in us. By this we know that we abide in Him, and He in us, because He has given us of His Spirit. And we have seen and testify that the Father has sent the Son as Savior of the world. Whoever confesses that Jesus is the Son of God, God abides in him, and he in God. And we have known and believed the love that God has for us. God is love, and he who*

abides in love abides in God, and God in him. Love has been perfected among us in this: that we may have boldness in the day of judgment; because He is, so are we in this world. There is no fear in love; but perfect love casts out fear, because fear involves torment. But he who fears has not been made perfect in love. We love Him because He first loved us. If someone says, "I love God," and hates his brother, he is a liar; for he who does not love his brother whom he has seen, how can he love God whom he has not seen? And this commandment we have from Him: that he who loves God must love his brother also (1 John 4:7-21).

Love remains at the forefront of God's work for the world. He proved His love by sending His Son Jesus Christ to free the world from enmity and rebellion, reconciling the world to Himself. Love is perfect. It relates all things in heaven and earth to one another peacefully and in a perfect way. There is no law against love. That is why Christians call Jesus the Prince of peace and love, because He chose to love His enemies contrary to what his enemies did to Him. With His love, Jesus is the real liberator of the world and He expresses the perfect law of liberty.

This is the example God Almighty desires the world to follow. He loves people and wants people to follow His footsteps by loving and respecting one another. God created people with love and for love in order to relate them to one another in the same way He relates Himself to His creatures. God created people in spiritual likeness to Himself and blessed them in His love so they could become His fruitful agents on earth (Genesis 1:26-28). That is why the essence and the central message of His word is love:

"You shall love the LORD your God with all your heart, with all your soul, and with all your mind." "This is the first and great commandment. "And the second is like it: You shall love your neighbor as yourself.' "On these two commandments

> *hang all the Law and the Prophets* (Matthew 22:37-39; also read Deuteronomy 5:21-22; 6:5).

These words challenge people to engage their minds and hearts in understanding the depth, height and width of love in order to discover the status of their soul in relation to God and His creatures. They show us whether we are related to God and whether we are fully enabled to relate to the world around us. They are to make us godly and friendly people. The whole philosophy of the Bible is that, if we unite with Jesus Christ, we will no longer be slaves to narrow-mindedness and separatist behaviors but we will be liberated in order to love God and to live in peace with His creatures.

Muslims, however, are not able to describe God in the same way that Christians do. The words of the Qur'an present Muslims as the ultimate community of God that must manifest the success of God through military or cultural forces. Radical Muslims draw their fighting spirit from the teachings of the Qur'an, Muhammad and his successors and fight their non-Muslim neighbors instead of loving them:

> *Believers! wage war against such of the infidels as are your neighbors, and let them find you rigorous: and know that God is with those who fear him* (Q.9:123).

> *Make war upon such of those to whom the Scriptures have been given as believe not in God, or in the last day, and who forbid not that which God and His Apostle have forbidden, and who profess not the profession of the truth, until they pay tribute out of hand, and they be humbled…The Jews say, "Ezra is a son of God"; and the Christians say, "the Messiah is a son of God."…God do battle with them! How are they misguided* (Q.9:29-30).

Forgiveness of Sin and Salvation

The misinformation Muslims have about Christian beliefs can be removed completely when the ambiguity of Muhammad's ministry and teaching about sin and the forgiveness is compared with the redemptive work of Jesus Christ.

Muhammad was ambiguous about a Muslim's future and in one instance he gave shocking news to Muslims that they would first be taken to hell:

> *... No soul can know what it will earn tomorrow...* (Q.31:34).

> *Man* (Muslims and non-Muslims) *saith: "What! after I am dead, shall I in the end be brought forth alive? Doth not man bear in mind that we made him at first, when he was nought? And I swear by the Lord, we will surely gather together them and the Satans: then will we set them on their knees round Hell: Then will we take forth from each band those of them who have been stoutest in rebellion against the God of Mercy: Then shall we know right well to who its burning is most due: No one is there of you who shall not go down unto it—this is a settled decree with thy Lord—Then will we deliver those who had the fear of God* [Muslims], *and the wicked will we leave in it on their knees"* (Q.19:66-72).

However, contrary to Muhammad's uncertainty, the Qur'an speaks of the certainty of Jesus Christ's ascension to heaven, known as paradise to the Muslim, a statement in line with the teachings of the Bible.

> *He was taken up into heaven* (Luke. 24:51).

Compared to:

> *Remember when God said, "O Jesus! verily I will cause thee to die, and will take thee up to myself and deliver thee from those who believe not"* (Q.3:55).

> *God took him up to Himself. And God is Mighty, Wise!* (Q.4:158).

Of some interest also is the qur'anic belief that the followers of Christ [Christians] hold a higher spiritual position than those who do not believe:

> *God said,...I will place those who follow thee* [Jesus] *above those who believe not, until the day of resurrection* (Q.3:55).

This qur'anic verse is a clear reflection of the many verses in the New Testament which testify to Jesus' saving power:

> *He* [God] *delivered us* [followers of the Son, Jesus Christ] *from the power of darkness and conveyed us into the kingdom of the Son of His love, in whom we have redemption, through His blood, the forgiveness of sins* (Colossians 1: 13-14; also read Luke 2:30-31; John 5:24).

Muslims, therefore, need to recognize Jesus Christ as the only One who truly rescued His followers from the dominion of hell. The Qur'an does not teach the same about Muhammad for Muslims. Why would a true prophet of God not be sure of his future state after death? This kind of uncertainty surely casts doubts on a religion claiming to be the best, last and most complete religion of all. If this is so, then why has a person been moved from a position of assurance in Christ, to one of doubt in Muhammad? This is not what you would expect if Muhammad was responding to the call of a caring and mighty God. The purpose of God in sending prophets is to call back people to Himself. If a prophet is not sure of his future, how then will he be a good example to other people? How can a prophet, not yet saved, be a bearer of God's divine message of salvation? How can an uncertain man become the messenger of certainty that he has not yet experienced himself? If God reveals His word to a person shouldn't he be sure of his destination? Is not God's message or mission all about creating assurance in the hearts of people? Why would someone submit himself to

God without this assurance? Doesn't submission to God carry with it admission to heaven?[1]

A true prophet of God must be someone who is certain of his own salvation and therefore can teach about the spiritual liberty he himself has tasted. In biblical faith not only the prophets, but also everyone who trusts in Christ the Son of God for deliverance from the bondage of sin, enjoys the certainty of salvation and freedom. They also become the voice of salvation for other people in the world. Those who enter into the covenant of righteousness and salvation with Jesus Christ through faith in Him are preserved for eternity in heaven and the power of hell will not overcome them:

> *And I* [Jesus] *say to you that you are Peter, and on this rock I will build My church, and the grates of Hades* [Hell] *shall not prevail against it* (Matthew 16:18).

> *Blessed are the pure in heart, for they shall see God* (Matthew 5:8).

> *And this is the testimony: that God has given us eternal life, and this life is in His Son. He who has the Son has life; he who does not have the Son of God does not have life….you who believe in the name of the Son of God … know that you have eternal life. Now this is the confidence we have in Him, that if we ask anything according to His will, He hears us. And if we know that He hears us-- whatever we ask--we know that we have the petition that we have asked of Him* (1 John 5:11-15).

---

1 Tradition states; when the time of Muhammad's prophetic mission arrived, three angels came down to him, split his stomach, filled it with wisdom and assurance and removed all doubts from him (Tabari, Muhammad-bin Jarir, *Tarikh-al-rosol val-molouk*, PP.853-4 and cf. Q.74:1-4). This is quite opposite to the uncertainty Muhammad felt, according to the Qur'an (Q.31:34; 46:9), years after his prophetic claim.

This is the major difference between the beliefs expounded in the Bible and those found in the Qur'an. Those who have built their faith upon the Qur'an are uncertain about their salvation. But those who have built their faith upon truth found in the Bible have the seal of God's salvation within them and have tasted the freedom that they will have forever.

God is holy. He cannot have a relationship with any unsaved and unrighteous person. He also cannot demand the unsaved and unrighteous person to act righteously unless He Himself saves the person from the dominion of darkness and grants them righteousness. How can an unsaved person who is in the dominion of sin act righteously to please God? How can we say a person is with God, or God is with a person while that individual is still in the bondage of sin and Satan? Those who have not been brought back to mankind's original state of relationship with God as a result of salvation through the Son Jesus Christ are totally separated from God. They might have a desire for God and a yearning to be united to God, but it does not mean that they have been reconciled to God or have a relationship with Him.

The Son of God?

The verses of the Qur'an about the sonship and deity of Christ contradict each other. The reason for this contradiction is that the Qur'an first borrowed from Christian traditions and Scriptures out of context, and second, it borrowed from other sources and arranged all these verses in such a way as to be very different from the Bible. However, it is obvious that the logic of the Qur'an's own verses does not reject the divinity of Jesus Christ. If Muslim scholars and evangelists would carefully consider and analyze the relevant Qur'anic verses theologically, they would not be able to deny the divinity of Jesus Christ.

God Had No Spouse

The Qur'an recounts the Christian doctrine that Jesus is the *Word* and the *Spirit* of God. It teaches that his birth was the result of the coming of the Word and Spirit of God upon the Virgin Mary, not as the result of a sexual relationship:

> *[W]hen angel said, "O Mary! Verily God announceth to thee the Word from Him: His name shall be, Messiah Jesus"* ... *She said, "How, o my Lord! shall I have a son, when man has not touched me?" He said, "Thus: God will create what He will;..."* (Q.3:45, 47).

> *The Messiah, Jesus, son of Mary, is only an apostle of God, and his Word which he conveyed into Mary, and a Spirit proceeding from him...* (Q.4.171b).

> *[W]e [God) sent our spirit to her [Mary), and he [Jesus) took before her the form of a perfect man* (Q.19:17).

> *And her who kept her maidenhood, and into whom we breathed of our spirit, and make her and her son a sign to all creatures* (Q.21:91).

These verses of the Qur'an appear to be more closely related to the Bible-based beliefs of Christians regarding Jesus' conception than to the many fanciful Islamic notions that have been floating around in the thoughts of Muslim evangelists throughout Islam's history. However, at the same time, the Qur'an accuses Christians of claiming that God had sexual relations with Mary in order to give birth to Jesus:

> *... Far be from His glory that He should have a son* (Q.4:171c).

> *Sole maker of the Heavens and of the Earth! How, when He hath no consort [spouse), should He have a son?...* (Q.6:101).

> *SAY: He is God alone: God the eternal! He begetteth not, and He is not begotten; And there is no like unto Him* (Q.112:1-4).

The concept of Mary being God's spouse as referred to here by the Qur'an is totally foreign to the pages of the Bible. The Bible clearly states that to be called the sons or daughters of God carries solely spiritual meaning:

Yet to all who received him, to those who believed in his name, he gave the right to become children of God – children born not of natural descent, nor of human decision or a husband's will, but born of God (John 1:12).

[You] have been born again, not of corruptible seed but incorruptible, through the word of God which lives and abides forever, because "All flesh is as grass, And all the glory of man as the flower of the grass. The grass withers, And its flower falls away, But the word of the LORD endures forever." (1 Peter 1:23-25).

That which is born of the flesh is flesh, and that which is born of the Spirit is spirit (John 3:6).

Although the previous Qur'anic verses suggest God would never have a son, the following verse of the Qur'an carries the meaning that God can have a son if He desires:

Had God desired to have had a son, he had surely chosen what he pleased out of his own creation. But praise be to Him! He is God, the One, the Almighty (Q.39:4).

The concept in the above verse is conditional: "If God desired to have had a son, He had . . ." This means that according to the Qur'an, it is not impossible for God to have a son. Although the possibility of God "having a son" threatens the teaching about the impersonal and unreachable god of the Qur'an, the Qur'an does not rule out the possibility of God having a son! This contradicts the Qur'an's own stand in cursing Jews and Christians for attributing fatherhood to God;

The Jews say, "Ezra (Ozair) is a son of God"; and the Christians say, "The Messiah is a son of God." Such the sayings in their mouths! They resemble the saying of the Infidels of old! God do battle with them! How are they misguided (Q.9:30).

The Son Incarnate!

The phrases the "Spirit of God" and the "Word of God" in the Qur'an (Q.4.171b; Q.19:17) carries the same meaning as

"God the Spirit" and "God the Word". When the Qur'an says that Jesus was born by the coming of the Spirit and the Word of God, it means, that Jesus was born by the coming of "God the Spirit and Word" upon the Virgin Mary. In other words, God became man. This was the belief of the prophets of the Bible who foretold the revelation of God through Jesus Christ many hundreds of years before Islam and Christianity. They stated that the Almighty God would dwell among humankind by way of a Virgin. Isaiah, the eight century B.C. prophet says:

> *Therefore the Lord Himself will give you a sign: Behold, the virgin shall conceive and bear a Son, and shall call His name Immanuel* [which means, "God with us"] (Isaiah 7:14).

> *For unto us a Child is born, unto us a Son is given; and the government will be upon His shoulder. And His name will be called Wonderful, Counselor, Mighty God, Everlasting Father, Prince of Peace. Of the increase of His government and peace there will be no end, upon the throne of David and over His kingdom, to order it and establish it with judgment and justice from that time forward, even forever* (Isaiah 9:6-7).

The New Testament says that these prophecies were fulfilled when the Word and the Spirit of God appeared in the flesh of Jesus Christ with the fullness of His power, glory and grace:

> *So all this was done that it might be fulfilled which was spoken by the Lord through the prophet, saying: "Behold, the virgin shall be with child, and bear a Son, and they shall call His name Immanuel," which translated, "God with us."* (Matthew 1:22-23).

> *In the beginning was the Word, and the Word was with God, and the Word was God. He was in the beginning with God. All things were made through Him, and without Him nothing was made that was made…And the Word became flesh and dwelt among us, and we beheld His glory, the glory as of the only begotten of the Father, full of grace and truth* (John 1:1-3,14).

Tabari, the notable ancient Islamic commentator and historian, narrated the visit of Mary, the mother of Christ, to Elizabeth, the mother of John the Baptist [*Yahya*), as following, which confirms the divinity of Christ. Mary asked Elizabeth, "do you know that I am pregnant?" Elizabeth answered, "the one that is in my womb bowed down to the one in your womb, this is the confirmation of the Word of God".[1] John who was not the word of God bowed down to the divine Word of God, Jesus.

Spirit and Substance

The Qur'an also believes that spirit can become flesh:

> *When they* [angels) *went in unto him* [Abraham) *and said, "Peace!"*...(Q.51:25 also 11:60; 15:52).

We learn from the Islamic tradition that the angel Gabriel appeared to Muhammad in various occasions as a man.[2]

The Qur'an again quotes the biblical narration that God showed Himself as fire (substance) to Moses:

> *Hath the history of Moses reached thee? When he saw a fire, ... he came to it, he was called to, "O Moses! Verily, I am thy Lord:... I am God: there is no God but me"*... (Q.20:9,11,12,14; also 28:29-30).

The Almighty God became a fire (a substance) and it did not seem blasphemous to the Qur'an. How then does it become blasphemous to the Qur'an when the Bible announces that God became flesh (substance)?

The word "man" (*nass* in Arabic) is highly valued in Islamic doctrine. When the word "Allah" is replaced by the word "man", the meaning of many verses in the Qur'an is no different. Would it not be more acceptable to Muslims for God to dwell in man than for Him to dwell in any other substance?

---

1 Tabari, Muhammad-bin Jarir, *Tarikh-al-rosol val-molouk*, P.518.

2 Tabari, Muhammad-bin Jarir, *Tarikh-al-rosol val-molouk*, PP.510,849,1082-3. & Ibn Hisham, *Sirat Rasul Allah*, PP.212-13. & A. M. A. Shahrestani, *Tozih-almelal*, P.62.

Does the kind of substance God chooses to dwell in make a difference for the Qur'an? If it does not, then why does the Qur'an blame Christians for claiming that God became man? And if it does make a difference, then why is it not more acceptable for Muslims when God chooses to dwell in the best of His creatures, man?[1] Isn't it man who is called to live under the rule of God? Isn't it man that is more precious to God than anything else? How can the Qur'an believe in the incarnation of Satan (who became a snake drawing people toward many kinds of curses), and yet not believe in the incarnation of God (who became a man to draw humankind to heaven)? Is God an aloof, indifferent, merciless being when it comes to saving humankind, compared to Satan who is present in every affair of humankind and tries to destroy them?

The Son the Creator

The Qur'an also unexpectedly attributes to Jesus the work of creation when it describes the life-giving power of Jesus to create a bird in the same manner and sequence that both the Qur'an and the Bible attribute to God:

> ...*Out of clay will I* [Jesus) *make for you, as it were, the figure of a bird: and I will breathe into it, and it shall become, by God's leave, a bird* (Q.3:49; cf. Q.5:110).

The breath that Jesus breathed into the clay bird had the same power and characteristics as the breath of God in creation. If Jesus is not divine, how can His breath act in the same way as does the divine breath? Did this breath come from inside of Jesus? Was that because God had made His full dwelling in Jesus? Doesn't the breath of creation belong only to God? Did that bird really join the world of living creatures, or was it only magic? The Qur'an says, it became a living bird,[2] --a bird that

---

1   According to Muslims' conviction, man is God's vicegerent or *khalifa* in Arabic (Q.2:30).

2   Tabari states in his, "*Commentary on the Qur'an*" (P.983) the bird that Jesus created was a "bat" and flies at night.

could become a testimony to the life-giving breath that came out of Jesus. Because of these verses and many others, the fact that the Qur'an denies the divinity of Jesus is something that brings the consistency of the Qur'an's theology into question.

Once in Harmony with the Bible

The start of Muhammad's life work was closely related to the Christian community. His protests against idol worshipers, who called the idols the children of Allah, stem back to the advice of his Christian relatives and friends who taught him that the deity and sonship of Christ was the truth, not idols:

> *You shall not make idols for yourselves; neither a carved image nor a sacred pillar shall you rear up for yourselves; nor shall you set up an engraved stone in your land, to bow down to it; for I am the LORD your God* (Leviticus 26:1).

> *The works of the flesh are evident, which are:: ... idolatry and...* (Galatians 5:19-20).

> *But to the Son He* [God] *says: "Your throne, O God, is forever and ever;...* (Hebrew 1:8).

Muhammad might not have understood the authenticity of the divinity and the sonship of Christ as the Bible describes it. However, he did not criticize or reject the idea in the first years of his friendly relationship with the churches. He was happy spending time with Christians and tried to prove that he was a friend, by adapting himself to their way of life. Otherwise, the church leaders in Mecca and Syria would not have been interested in supporting him. His respect toward Jesus as "Messiah (Christ), Word and Spirit of God" was proof of his eagerness in his early years of ministry, to place himself in line with the Bible's prophets who all willingly bowed to the coming God, as "Messiah and the Son of God" (Isaiah 7:14; 9:6-7; Matthew 16:16; John 1:1-3,14; cf. Q.4:171).

The titles "Messiah" and "the Word and the Spirit of God"[1] in the Bible are all attributed to Jesus because of His pre-eminent and superior characteristics among all creatures. It is incomprehensible that Muhammad was once in harmony with the Bible, with the prophets of the Bible and with influential Christian leaders, but at the same time denied the deity and sonship of Jesus Christ. He was with those Christians who believed in Jesus as "God, the Word and the Spirit of God, the Messiah and the Son of God". There is no evidence of Muhammad denying the above in his early ministry.

In addition to the above, the Biblical and Talmudic backgrounds of the Qur'an[2] are also proof of Muhammad's willingness to follow the faith of the Christian leaders with who he was in close contact. Even though in his later ministry he fell into enmity with Christians and Jews, he still could not erase the biblical flavor of his message that was there from the beginning. We see that he overwhelmingly tried to keep his message related to the Bible. Even in his exaltation, he still related himself to the Jews. He exalted himself above the Jewish prophets when he introduced himself as the seal of all the prophets descended from the Jews:

> ...*the unlettered Prophet whom they* [Jews) *shall find described with them in the Law and Evangel...*(Q.7:157; cf. Q.61:6).
>
> *Muhammad is...the seal of the prophets* (Q.33:40).

All the evidence shows that from the beginning, Muhammad was in harmony with the Christian leaders and consequently, in favor of the deity and sonship of Christ. However, this did not remain so. The changing characteristics of his political faith caused him to lose his Christian environment after his flee from Mecca to Medina. The Islamic tradition clearly proves that in

---

1 For further information read, J. Gilchrist, *The Title of Jesus in the Qur'an and the Bible,* England: Roodepoort Mission Press, 1986.

2 A. I. Katsh, *Judaism and the Koran,* New York: A. S. Barnes and Company, Inc., 1962, all pages.

Medina during his confrontation with the Christian leaders, he totally denied the sonship and the deity of Christ.[1] He had gained great power from his new movement in Medina.

No longer was he known as just a prophet anymore, as he was in Mecca, but greater than all and the seal of all. The religion he had created was also called superior to all other religions. Therefore, he could not call Jesus the Son of God anymore and he had to deal with all the Bible's teaching that were contrary to what he was asserting.

Supreme Characteristics of the Son

The Son Jesus Christ, the Bible says, is God, greater than the angels and the prophets:

- The Son is alive from eternity to eternity and He is the exact representation of God's being and over all creation (John 1:1-3,14,18; 17:5; Hebrews 1:3; Colossians 1:15; Revelation 11:15).
- The Son proves His equality with God (the Father) by the unique words and works He speaks and accomplishes (Matthew 5:43-48; Luke 7:16; John 5:21-30; 11:38-39, 43-44). Whatever God does the Son does also (John. 5:19).
- The Son is greater than every prophet, greater than Abraham, Jacob, Moses, David, Solomon, Jonah, John the Baptist (John 8:53,56-58; 4:12-14; 5:46; Hebrews 3:5-6; Matthew 22:43; Luke 11:31-32; John 1:29-30).
- The Son is "love" and, therefore, is for all humankind (1 John 4:7; John 3:16).
- The Son became the unchangeable standard and eternal glory for Moses who, for the sake of the Son Jesus Christ as one of greater value, chose to be mistreated rather than to enjoy the pleasure of the kingdom of Egypt (Hebrews 11:24-26; Matthew 17:3).

---

1 Ibn Hisham, *Sirat Rasul Allah*, PP.509-12.

- The Son became the climax of all the prophecies in the Bible (Acts 10:43).
- The Son is from heaven whereas all other prophets are from the dust of the earth (John 3:13; 6:38,42,62; 8:23; 16:28; 1Corinthians 15:47; cf. Q.19:17).
- The Son came down from heaven to take the lost back to his/her original state. This is what the prophets and the law could not do (Acts 4:12; Galatians 2:16).
- The Son, contrary to the prophets, is called the Word and the Spirit of God (John 1:1-3; Luke 1:35; cf. Q.4:171).
- The Son is *the way Himself* to heaven (John 14:6) whereas the prophets are only indicators to the way.
- The Son has power to lay down His life for many and take it again (John 10:18). Adam satisfied his sinful nature and in this way spiritual death came to all humankind, but Jesus satisfied the nature of God, laid down His life for all humankind and once again brought life to humankind (Romans 5:15-21).
- The Son appeared to destroy the devil's work and to bridge the gap between God and humankind (1 John 3:8; Colossians 1:20; Matthew 4:1-11) whereas no one prophet was able to do so.
- The Son has victory over sin, death and Satan (Hebrews 2:14; John 16:33).
- The Son can bring the dead bodies to life (John 11:43-44; cf. Q.5:110).
- The Son is greater than the angels and all angels worship Him (Hebrews 1:4,6).
- The Son is alive and in heaven and rules over His people from heaven (Colossians 1:18).
- The Son provided the opportunity for humankind to have access to eternal life, which Adam deprived them of (Genesis 3:24; Revelation 22:14).
- The Son is the eternal source of salvation for all who believe in and follow Him (Luke 2:31; 1 Jn. 1:7-9). He breaks the power of sin in everyone's life from the moment one

believes in Him, thus being assured of his/her salvation (Luke 7:48-49; John 5:24; 1 John 5:13).

- The Son's message cannot be under the influence of the fluctuating "yes" and "no" of worldly politics. Instead, His "yes" was always "yes" and His "no" was always "no" (Matthew 5:37; 2 Corinthians 1:18-22).

- The Son did not come to be served, but to serve, and to give his life as a ransom for many (Matthew 20:28).

- The Son is interested in a relationship with humankind in order to save them. He knows that everybody's heart cries for freedom. He, therefore, does not exclude anyone from His plan of salvation (John 3:16-17; Romans 3:23-26).

- The Son is the light of the *world* (John 8:12; cf. Q.3:3-4; 19:21).

- The Son knows the future (Luke 18:31-32).

- The Son will come again with glory to judge the world (1 Thessalonians 4:16; Matthew 16:27; John 5:28-29; cf.Q.43:61).

- The Son has come and given us understanding that we may know the true God (2 John 5:20).

The above qualities are supremely above the characteristics of all humankind. They are heavenly qualities which supersede all earthly qualities. They are those qualities that only the Heavenly Ruler and King can possess. One must be God to have these qualities. These qualities do not fit with Muhammad's hypothesis in which he, as a man, tries to provide a purely "of this world" explanation for Jesus Christ. These qualities are heavenly characteristics that can only be revealed and described by the Spirit of God. Humankind can understand it only when they open their ears to hear the words of the Holy Spirit. As Jesus described to His students, the meaning of the term "the Son" cannot be revealed by man but only by His Father in heaven:

> *"Who do you say I* [Jesus] *am?" Simon Peter answered and said, "You are the Christ, the Son of the living God." Jesus*

*answered and said to him, "Blessed are you Simon Bar- Jonah,
for flesh and blood has not revealed this to you, but my Father
who is in heaven"* (Matthew 16:15-17).

On the other hand, we can see these qualities are far beyond the
objectives of Muhammad's ministry. They are the qualities of
a sacrificial ministry that lays down divine life so all may come
to realize love as being the most fundamental tool in unifying
the nations of the world in One God:

> *For God so loved the world that He gave His only begotten
> Son, that whoever believes in Him should not perish but have
> everlasting life* (John 3:16).

These qualities were beyond Muhammad's power and he could
not show them in his ministry. For the success of his political
movement, Muhammad, therefore, had no choice but to reject
the sonship of Jesus Christ, and to introduce Him as somebody
lesser than he was. The sonship of Christ did not go along
with the greatness of Muhammad's worldly political power.
Therefore, he had to reduce Jesus Christ and introduce himself
as someone greater than Jesus.

The Son Reconciles People to God

The Son, for Christians and for Jews (the coming Messiah), is
greater than anyone on the earth, including Muhammad. But
in the Qur'an the Son is not given this status. In the Bible, the
Son is from heaven and can reconcile humankind to God by
rescuing us from the dominion of Satan and taking us to his
heavenly kingdom:

> *He* [God] *has delivered us from the power of darkness and
> conveyed us into the kingdom of the Son of His love … For it
> pleased the Father that in Him* [the Son] *all the fullness should
> dwell, and by Him to reconcile all things to Himself, by Him,
> whether things on earth or things in heaven, having made
> peace through the blood of His cross* (Colossians 1:13,19-20).

In other words, the Son takes people, whom Satan has separated from God, back to Him. There is no one except the Son Jesus Christ who can take people back to their original state. That is why Jesus said:

> *I am the way, the truth and the life. No one comes to the Father except through Me* (John 14:6).

This truth is not taught in the Qur'an. So the actual difference between the Qur'an and the Bible is nothing other than the two quite different positions and roles attributed to Jesus Christ. In the Bible Jesus Christ holds a position as the supreme life-saver from heaven and in this way makes the Bible different from the Qur'an.

Teaching on the Crucifixion

There are two different statements about the death and crucifixion of Jesus in the Qur'an and tradition[1]:

One statement refers to God's plan to put Jesus to death and thereafter to take Him back to heaven:

> *Remember when God said, "O Jesus! verily I will cause thee to die, and will take thee up to myself and deliver thee from those who believe not"* (Q.3:55).

> *And the peace of God was on me* [Jesus] *the day I was born, and will be the day I shall die, and the day I shall be raised to life* (Q.19: 33).

But there is an opposing statement in the Qur'an, that says Jesus was neither killed nor crucified but simply taken to God:

> *And for their saying, "Verily we have slain the Messiah, Jesus the son of Mary, and Apostle of God." Yet they slew him not, and they crucified him not, but they had only his likeness. And they who differed about him were in doubt concerning him: No sure knowledge had they about him, but followed only an*

---

1 Tabari, Muhammad-bin Jarir, *Tarikh-al-rosol val-molouk*, PP.520-21.

opinion, and they did not really slay him, but God took him up to Himself. And God is Mighty, Wise! (Q.4:157-158).

The footnote of the editor of an ancient Muslim scholar's book also confirms the death of Christ by referring to three first-century, non-Christian historians, Josephus, Tacitus (Tacit) and Suetonius (Suetone).[1]

However, in describing the life of Jesus Christ on earth, Muslims rely on Q.4:157-158. They do not believe that Jesus was crucified or that Jesus died on the Cross for the sin of all people before rising again. They do believe that one of those who plotted to kill Jesus died in his place. They state that God took Jesus into heaven at that time and changed another man's face to look like Jesus. Although the man was shouting that he was not Jesus, no one listened to him and he was substituted for Jesus and put to death on the Cross.

Muslims believe Muhammad is too holy to be likened by men. An example is when Muslims did not allow Hollywood to show Muhammad's face in the film, "*Muhammad, the Apostle of Allah*". Considering that the Qur'an introduced Jesus as sinless and greatest among all the prophets, including Muhammad, why would Muslims venerate Muhammad and not Jesus? What was the purpose of making a Jesus look-alike die and taking the unique Jesus to heaven? Wouldn't it have been better for God not to deceive people but rather kill off His enemies and take Jesus to heaven before the eyes of the people?

As we are aware from the Church history, the idea of the substitution of somebody else for Christ on the Cross is not unique to Islam. In fact, it goes back to centuries before Islam. From the second century AD, some people said that Jesus could not have been crucified and that somebody else was crucified in his place.

---

1 Shahrestani, A. M. A., *Tozih-almelal*, P.316 of book1.

There are many reasons for why these substitution legends are not historically credible:[1]

- The Gospel says that Jesus was crucified.
- There are extra-biblical testimonies about the death of Christ.
- There is not a shred of first-century testimony to the contrary by friend or foe of Christianity.
- The legends ignore the participation of Jesus' disciples, and of the Romans who crucified Him.

Muslims denial of Christ's death by crucifixion is therefore based on their misunderstandings of biblical theology.

This belief by Muslims that Jesus went straight into heaven, still raises some theological questions which may help Muslims to realize some great facts about Jesus: Why would Jesus, and not Muhammad as the seal of prophets, be taken to the heavenly place to be with God? Why would Muhammad not be certain about himself being one day with God, whereas he was about Jesus?:

> *SAY: I have no control over what may be helpful or hurtful to me, but as God willeth. Had I the knowledge of his secrets, I should revel in the good, and evil should not touch me...* (Q.7:188).

> *SAY: I am no apostle of new doctrines: neither know I what will be done with me or you...* (Q.46:9).

If Muhammad was the seal of the prophets, why wasn't he sure of being in heavenly places like Jesus who, according to Muslims, is a lesser prophet who was not able to complete the work of God on earth? Why did he not have the same hope and assurance as the prophets of the Bible? If he was not an apostle of a new doctrine and was following the same doctrine that the Son Jesus Christ followed, he should have been assured

---

1 Read N.L. Geisler & A. Saleeh, PP.280-6.

about his and his followers' salvation just like the followers of Christ:

> *And this is the testimony: that God has given us eternal life, and this life is in His Son. He who has the Son has life; he who does not have the Son of God does not have life* (1 John 5:11-12).

This is the confidence that the followers of the Son Jesus Christ have in their approach to God. The verbs "has given" and "has" in the verses above imply the assurance of salvation that they have in this life on earth. Muhammad himself also was aware of the certainty of salvation that comes by following Jesus Christ when he said:

> *God said,…I will place those who follow thee* [Jesus] *above those who believe not, until the day of resurrection* (Q.3:55-56).

Why would the Qur'an assert such a righteous position for the followers of Jesus but not for the followers of Muhammad? What is it that has made the name "Jesus" a name that is above all other prophets? It is nothing other than the doctrine of "the death and the resurrection of Jesus" that can provide the right answer to these questions. The atoning death and resurrection of Jesus Christ is the central theme of the Bible and it is this that has provided assurance of salvation for people. It opens the door of eternal life to humankind and brings them back to their original state of righteousness, reconciling them to one another and to God. The Cross is the basis of God's plan to destroy the wall of hostility among people and between them and God. The Apostle Paul was initially one of the strictest enemies of Christians, and Jesus revealed Himself to him, thereby changing his life. The following words prove the life-changing power of the Gospel of Jesus Christ in Paul's life;

> *Now all things are of God, who has reconciled us to Himself through Jesus Christ, and has given us the ministry of reconciliation* (2 Corinthians 5:18).

And by Him [Jesus Christ, the Son] *to reconcile all things to Himself, by Him, whether things on earth or things in heaven, having made peace through the blood of His cross* (Colossians 1:20).

Eternal Death versus the Death of Christ

It is not only the Son Jesus Christ that knows the secrets of the kingdom of heaven. They are also revealed to those who follow Him. Through the atoning death of the Son, the followers of the Son also become the children of the kingdom of heaven. The simple and understandable logic that lies behind being the children of God is that nothing of the kingdom of heaven is hidden to its children. The children are not strangers. They know their heavenly Father's secrets. The death of the Son on the Cross and His resurrection from the dead have changed the spiritual identity of His followers. They have been moved from the kingdom of Satan to the kingdom of heaven so that they can share in the knowledge and advantages of eternal life.

The death of the Son on the Cross is the sacrifice of God for the sin of the world. The resurrection of the Son is the victory of God over the eternal death of Satan. Eternal life is for those who are accepted and included in the price paid by God for our sin and share in the victory gained by Him through the Son Jesus Christ. In fact, this is the major difference between the Qur'an and the Bible. The words of the Qur'an do not reveal that any price was paid so that humankind could come back to God, and yet this theme is central in the Bible's revelation. The death of Jesus Christ is the necessary sacrifice for the sins of the world and His resurrection is the victory over eternal death. The theology of the Old and New Testaments is based upon the promise and realization of these events:

All we like sheep have gone astray; We have turned, every one, to his own way; And the LORD has laid on Him [the Son] *the iniquity of us all. Yet it pleased the LORD to bruise Him; He has put Him to grief. When You make His soul an offering for sin, He shall see His seed, He shall prolong His days, and the pleasure of the LORD shall prosper in His hand. He shall see the labor of His soul, and be satisfied. By His knowledge My righteous Servant shall justify many, for He shall bear their iniquities* (Isaiah 53:6, 10-11).

Who was delivered up [to death] *because of our offenses, and was raised because of our justification* (Romans 4:25).

Who Himself [the Son] *bore our sins in His own body on the tree, that we, having died to sins, might live for righteousness – by whose stripes you were healed. For you were like sheep going astray but have now returned to the Shepherd and Overseer of you souls* (1 Peter 2:24-25).

The Finished Work of Christ

We know from the Qur'an that Muhammad blamed the Jews for the killing of the prophets. Why was it difficult for Muhammad to believe that the Jews also killed Jesus since He is called a prophet in the Qur'an? What happened so that he changed his mind about Jesus' death and said that he never truly died? He might have heard about "the finished work of Christ on the Cross" from the contemporary Christians around him, and for that reason, he might have changed his mind. Why? Because the finished work of Christ on the Cross, in a sense, stands in opposition to Muhammad's assertion that his ministry was the final fulfillment of the prophetic task. This certainly could be one reason for him rejecting the teaching about the Cross. Another reason might have been the fact that in Islam Jesus was called one of the five great prophets: Noah, Abraham, Moses, Jesus and Muhammad. If the powerful Muslim prophet and political leader confirmed that the tiny Jewish nation had dared to kill the greatest prophet, Jesus (who was considered to be the same rank as Muhammad), it would have been very discouraging for the politico-religious army of Islam. This might have in turn led Muhammad to claim that the Jews were able to kill the minor prophets only, but not the ones in whom

God placed so much love. Alternatively, Muhammad might have been discouraged by the Roman political belief that any crucified person had to be a criminal and therefore Christians worshipped a criminal and his cross. This kind of political belief opposes the religious values of Islam that assert that a prophet is holy and cannot be a criminal.

Righteousness through the Sacrifice of Christ

The philosophy that lies behind the crucifixion of the Son Jesus Christ is crucial to Christianity. Just as the descendants of Adam became unrighteous through his rebellious example, so also through the sacrifice of Jesus Christ on the Cross many who follow Him will be made righteous (See Romans 5:19). Why did Jesus undertake this task? It was because God loved the world and wanted to have many in the world back in His kingdom. What Jesus did on the Cross was the result of God's love, justice and holiness directed toward the sinful world. This act made salvation available for the world.

Any understanding about Jesus is based on the relationship between the Cross and the forgiveness of sin in the Bible. Although Muhammad at some stages of his ministry accepted the truth about the death and the resurrection of Jesus Christ (Q.3:55; 19:33), he rejected it later on in his ministry and substituted something else in its place that could suit the progress of Islam (Q.4:157-158; 5:117).

Because of his political fame, Muhammad missed the real desire of God that the spiritual confidence was more important than worldly fame. God's goal is to establish eternal life and righteousness in people's hearts by driving out Satan of their hearts so that they can have relationship with Him. A fallen man is not able to release himself from Satan and establish eternal life and righteousness in his own heart, but God is able to release him. Rituals do not plant the Spirit of God in the hearts of people and cannot save them from Satan, but God can and does. On the other hand, God does not leave salvation up to humankind, as He is the only power to overcome Satan and establish justice and righteousness in the hearts of people. Also, justice, holiness, righteousness, love and peace are the very needs of the practical life on earth and are to be established in the hearts of people on earth so that they can have peaceful relationships with God and each other. On the other hand, if people are crying for or desiring God's peace, justice, holiness, salvation, care, love and mercy now, why shouldn't God meet their present needs now, instead of leaving them for the life after? Christ came to meet our needs now and forever:

> *Having disarmed principalities* [or spiritual forces of evil in Ephesians 6:12], *He* [God] *made a public spectacle of them, triumphing over them in it* [cross] (Colossians 2:15).

> *The Son of God was manifested, that He might destroy the works of the devil* (1 John 3:8b).

God manifested Himself in Jesus in order to destroy the work of Satan and establish His justice in the hearts of nations (Matthew 12:20-21), and create peace among nations and between nations and Himself (Colossians 1:20).

Teaching on Morality

No Potential Standard for Moral Values

Muslims claim to have moral supremacy over other nations, but in reality they are unable to have an absolute moral code for such a claim. Theologically speaking, Islam cannot have a Moral Standard from the true God since God was introduced to them as an impersonal and unknowable God. Such a teaching creates a wall between them and God and makes His truth or the goodness, as a potential standard for moral values, unknowable and inaccessible. Therefore, it will be irrational to claim any moral supremacy over others without having an absolute moral code. Not only this, Muslims will also be unable to take their Islamic moral codes as measuring tools for evaluating the authenticity of other values since Allah has not revealed himself and no none is able to know whether he is good or not.

Also, a brief scrutiny of what the Qur'an teaches about life and afterlife proves that an Islamic lifestyle cannot be a good moral example for the world. According to the Qur'an, Muslims are not saved and in the kingdom of heaven (or paradise) in their life on earth. An unsaved person, who is not a part of God's household, is unable to be more trustworthy than the followers of other religions who have the same spiritual position. Only those, who are in the kingdom of heaven, can be good examples of godly living for others. It is possibly because of Christians' assurance of salvation that the Qur'an itself exalts the followers of Jesus Christ above others as perfect examples. Consider the following verse from the Qur'an:

> God said…I will place those who follow thee [Jesus] above those who believe not, until the day of resurrection (Q.3:55-56).

The word "above" in this verse points to the Christian victory over ungodliness which is received through the faith in Jesus Christ. Islam does not offer such a perfect and victorious life through obedience to Muhammad or submission to Allah. For this reason, Islam cannot be called "The Perfect Religion". Muslims call Islam "The Perfect Religion" because Muhammad said so, but such a claim does not match the doctrine of Islam. Towards the end of his mission, Muhammad showed fully political and made all other aspects of life, including spirituality, subject to his politics and in this way kept himself away from Christians, rejected the spiritual superiority of Christ and claimed Islam's and Muslims' superiority over others.[1] As a result, Islam became a political religion, and its author, Allah, revealed his verses or abrogated the previous ones if they were convenient for Muhammad's politics.

---

1 Q.3:110

Another reason to reject the superiority of Islam over the faith in Christ is the two opposite spiritual stands that Muhammad and Jesus hold toward sin. According to the Qur'an, Jesus is sinless but Muhammad is a sinner. Therefore, the example of Jesus, introduced in the Qur'an, is godly and better than the example of Muhammad. For this reason, Muhammad's claim on calling himself the seal of all prophets contradicts the highest spiritual position the Qur'an attributes to Jesus. Muhammad also claimed that Jesus foretold his coming in the Gospel. This cannot be true too. Because Jesus, as the sinless and perfect model, would never want to recommend a sinner, Muhammad, to people as someone who could bring all other religion to completion. In other words, Jesus would never want to leave His perfect and completed ministry into the hands of someone who is not cleansed of his sins and is not in a perfect relationship with God.

If a person is not dressed with the assurance of salvation, like the true followers of Jesus Christ, s/he is not able to become a good example for others. Paul, the disciple of Jesus Christ, said:

> *Our citizenship is in heaven.* [Our] *names are in the book of life.* (Philippians 3:20a; 4:3c).

> *God, who is rich in mercy, because of His great love with which He loved us, … raised us up together, and made us sit together in the heavenly place in Christ Jesus … Now, therefore, you are no longer strangers and foreigners, but fellow citizens with the saints and members of the household of God* (Ephesians 2:4,6).

For this reason, the Gospel of Christ calls His followers, the *salt* and *light* of the world (Matthew 5:13,14). Without Jesus and His Cross, no amount of effort will produce such moral lives that are pleasing to God and blessing to the world.

The Breath of Debauchery

The criticism by Muslim evangelists of the Christian faith becomes more illogical when the author of their own faith, Allah, has corrupted Satan and ordained men and women to be sinners:

> *He* [Satan or Iblis] *said: "Because thou hast thrown me out of the way, lo! I will lie in wait for them on thy straight way:. . ."* (Q.7:16)

> [Iblis] *said: "O my Lord! because Thou hast put me in the wrong, I will make (wrong) fair-seeming to them on the earth, and I will put them all in the wrong* (Q.15:39)

> *And* [Allah] *breathed into it* (human soul) *its wickedness* [in Arabic debauchery] *and its piety* (Q.91:8).

> *Allah created man in toil and trouble* (Q.90:4).

Allah himself created Satan as a corrupt being and foe for people and also created humanity in sin, toil and trouble so that people will not be able to escape immorality. Since Allah has inspired sin, which is stealing, lying, adultery, killing, etc., then can the call of Allah upon his followers lead them to peace and truth? Absolutely not. If Allah is the cause of every lawless act, you will not expect from his followers to be good or to do good.

Such works do not match with the nature of the God of the Bible, which says:

> *God did not call us to uncleanness, but in holiness* (1 Thessalonians 4:7).

> *The wisdom that is from above is first* **pure**; *then peaceful, gentle, willing to yield, full of mercy and good fruit, without partiality and without hypocrisy* (James 3:17).

Islam and the god of Islam will not be able to help people to distinguish between truth and untruth. For this reason, an action in Islam can be moral in a particular situation but immoral in another. Muslims cannot escape the immorality which Allah has breathed in them.

The Privileges for Beloved Men

Allah is the creator and cause of corruption in Islam. If Allah was not able to keep himself away from sin, can his followers stay away from immorality? The answer is "no". For this reason, we find embarrassing documents from Muslim leaders. They have documented copious words about the private parts of females (as young as infants), talking about them as if they are objects and not human beings.[1]

We also learn from the Qur'an itself that women are not compelled to guard their private parts from their fathers, father-in-laws, their own sons or stepsons, brothers, nephews, slaves or even their sterilized male attendants. They also can show their private parts to children who have not yet shown any interest in women's nakedness:

> *And speak to the believing women that they refrain their eyes, and observe continence; and that they display not their ornaments, except those which are external; and that they throw their veils over their bosoms, and display not their ornaments, except to their husbands or their fathers, or their husbands' fathers, or their sons, or their husbands' sons, or their brothers, or their brothers' sons, or their sisters' sons, or their women, or their slaves, or male domestics who have no natural force, or to children who note not women's nakedness. And let them not strike their feet together, so as to discover their hidden ornaments. And be ye all turned to God, O ye Believers! that it may be well with you* (Q.24:31).

The Arabic verse of the Qur'an uses the word "*foroujahonna*" which clearly implies the private and sexual parts of women below the waist. The word "foroujahonna" comes before the word "ornaments" in the verse. Rather than using the exact

---

1 Refer to the book: R. Khomeini, *Tahrirolvasyleh,* Iran/Ghom: Darol Elm, 1990.

meaning of the Arabic word within this specific passage of the Quran, the majority of translations into other languages use much milder words. In English, words such as "private parts" or "abstinence" are used. Moreover the word "farj" (the singular of the term "foroujahanna") is used in reference to Mary, Jesus' mother, in Q.66:12 (and also Q.21:91), referring to her private parts: the angel Jibril (Gabriel) is said to have breathed into Mary's vulva when allegedly causing Jesus to be conceived.

The following is from the Nobel Qur'an translation, which uses the two words "private parts" but places them inside brackets, trying to deceive the readers that it is not Allah's words:

> *And tell the believing women lower their gaze* [from looking at forbidden things, and protect their private parts from illegal sexual acts, etc.] *and not to show their adornment except that only which is apparent* [like palms of hands or one eye or both eyes for necessity to see the way, or outer dress like veils or gloves, head covering, apron, etc.], *to draw their veils all over Juyubihinna* [i.e. their bodies, faces, necks and bosoms, etc.] *and not to reveal their adornments except to their husbands, their fathers, their husbands' fathers, their sons, their husbands' sons, their brothers, or their brothers' sons, or their sisters' sons, or their* [Muslim] *women* [i.e. their sister in Islam], *or the* [female] *slaves whom their right hands possess, or old male servants who lack vigour, or small children who have no sense of the shame of sex. And let them not stamp their feet so as to reveal what they hide of their adornment. And all of you beg Allah to forgive you all, O Believer, that you may be successful* (Q.24:31).

So, this verse of the Qur'an says that women are not compelled to guard their private parts from some of their relative men. If the Qur'an teaches women to neglect protecting their private parts from most male relatives and others around them, how is it possible for people to escape sexual immorality? Where in the Christian Scriptures does it teach any woman to show naked and exhibit her private parts to other family members and relatives as is taught in the Qur'an? These types of words and thoughts would be embarrassing and shocking to the least caring inhabitants of many societies, even among those that do not believe in any religion or religious restrictions. Isn't immorality among close relatives often exposed in many societies as an abomination? Consider a city or village whose population is only made up of those relatives and other people who are mentioned in the above verse. If women in the streets of that city or village were encouraged to follow the teaching of the Qur'an, how would they be looked upon? What kind of moral messages would the children of the families from that village or city take out to the rest of the world?

This negligence about protecting the private parts of females has led to big problems among some devoted Muslim families. Islamic religious leaders have unavoidably always included instructions in their guide books (*Tozih Almasael*) about how to handle the circumstances when a man commits adultery with his aunts or has sexual intercourse with a man in his extended family. Khomeini wrote the following:[1]

- If a man before marrying the daughters of his paternal or maternal aunt commits adultery with their mothers, he cannot marry them anymore (subject 2394).
- If after marriage he has not yet had a sexual relationship with his wife (parental or maternal cousin) but has committed adultery with his mother-in-law (aunt), there is no disorder or harm done to their marriage (subject 2395).
- If he commits adultery with a women, he must not marry her daughter, but if he marries a lady, sleeps with her, and then commits adultery with her mother, his wife is still legitimate to him, and also if after marriage yet not having slept with his wife, he commits adultery with his mother-in-law, it is recommended (not compulsory) to divorce his wife (subject 2396).

---

1   Khomeini, R., *Tozih Almasael*, PP.379-80.

- If a man has married the mother or sister or the daughter of another man, and then had a sexual relationship with him, the marriage is still legitimate (subject 2406).

Surely sexual morality should be taught first in the family. God set a moral example when He took the initiative to clothe Adam and Eve so that their private parts were covered even at a time when they had no children and relatives. How could Muslim scholars claim to be morally better than Christians when the contents of the above verse (Q.24:31) are called shameful by the Bible? Why would it call Christians and Jews to forgo their most honorable family laws to join the Muslim community that provides the least protection for women? How could the Qur'an call the Muslim community the best community that has been produced for humankind?:

> *Ye* [Muslims] *are the best folk that hath been raised up unto mankind. Ye enjoin the Just, and ye forbid the Evil, and ye believe in God: And if the people of the Book had believed, it had surely been better for them! Believers there are among them, but most of them are perverse* (Q.3:110).

For sure, nominal Muslim men and women would also call the contents of the verse Q.24:31 shameful. The world already feels sad for the Muslim women who have been degraded in such an immoral way. The world should also feel pity for the wives of Muhammad who were called by Muhammad the mothers of Muslim nations, but treated carelessly in front of the eyes of their so-called Muslim children. Aisha, one of Muhammad's wives, said:

> *A person asked the Messenger of Allah about one who has sexual intercourse with his wife and parts away (without orgasm) whether bathing is obligatory for him. 'Aisha was sitting by him. The Messenger of Allah said: I and she (the Mother the Faithful) do it and then take a bath.*[1]

---

1 Muslim :: Book 3 :: Hadith 685

After the death of Muhammad, Muslim men went to Muhammad's wives directly and asked questions about sexual intercourse. They could send their wives to them in order to get the responses for their questions, but they did not because Muhammad had not set a good example for them:

> *Abu Musa reported: There cropped up a difference of opinion between a group of Muhajirs (Emigrants and a group of Ansar (Helpers) (and the point of dispute was) that the Ansar said: The bath (because of sexual intercourse) becomes obligatory only-when the semen spurts out or ejaculates. But the Muhajirs said: When a man has sexual intercourse (with the woman), a bath becomes obligatory (no matter whether or not there is seminal emission or ejaculation). Abu Musa said: Well, I satisfy you on this (issue). He (Abu Musa, the narrator) said: I got up (and went) to 'A'isha and sought her permission and it was granted, and I said to her: O Mother, or Mother of the Faithful, I want to ask you about a matter on which I feel shy. She said: Don't feel shy of asking me about a thing which you can ask your mother, who gave you birth, for I am too your mother. Upon this I said: What makes a bath obligatory for a person? She replied: You have come across one well informed! The Messenger of Allah (may peace be upon him) said: When anyone sits amidst four parts (of the woman) and the circumcised parts touch each other a bath becomes obligatory.[1]*

All these happened to women in the time of Muhammad and his successors, which are narrated in the pages of the Qur'an or Hadiths, are unfortunately to fulfill the immoral and fleshly desires of Muslim men. Even many of the corrupted nations of the world would never publicly accept such a dishonoring attitude against women. How can Muslim scholars and fundamentalists introduce Muhammad to others as a perfect moral example?

---

1 Muslim :: Book 3 :: Hadith 684

The following are some other examples that the Qur'an records of abuses against women that have been carried on around the world:

- Allah permitted Muhammad to marry the wife of his own adopted son, Zaid, after he caused his adopted son to divorce his wife. The Qur'an clearly states that Muhammad was planning in his heart to have her for himself while she was not yet divorced. However, Allah unveiled the plan for the privilege of his beloved prophet and let the plan be fulfilled (Q.33:37).[1] In the same chapter (sura), the Qur'an insists that Muhammad's companions must not marry his wives and therefore trouble his heart (Q.33:53).

- Allah permitted Muhammad to have any believing woman who gave herself up to him (Q.33:50).[2]

- Muhammad and his wives did not have an honest relationship with each other (Q.66:1-2).[3]

- In selecting his wives, Muhammad's overriding focus was on the outward appearance of girls and ladies rather than a sincere love. He divorced his new wives after having his private time with them and noticing that they were not as young as he expected or seeing stains on their skins (cf. Q.33:52).[4]

- The Qur'an allows child-marriage (Q.65:4). Though Muhammad was over fifty, he preferred to marry very young girls. He married a girl, called Aisha, at the age of six.[5]

- Allah allows Muslims to exchange one wife for another (Q.4:20) or replace one with the better one (Q.66:5).

- Muslim men were encouraged to possess the enslaved girls and take the enslaved mothers for themselves (Q.4:24;

---

1 Also, read: Muhammad-bin Jarir Tabari, *Tarikh-al-rosol val-molouk*, PP.1064-6.

2 Examples: Ibid., PP.1103,1297-9.

3 More examples: Ibid. PP.1294-1298.

4 Ibid., PP.1296-7.

5 Ibid., PP.930-3,1290-2.

33:52), ignoring the love and dependency they had toward their children and husbands.

- The judgment of the Qur'an is quiet toward Muslims who force their female slaves into prostitution in order to gain more money (Q.24:33).
- Men are superior to women and they have the right to beat and leave them alone in their beds if they oppose their husbands' desires (Q.4:34: 38:44).

Even the pre-Islamic Arab pagans did not abuse women as Muslims did. The Qur'an acknowledges that there was a pre-Islamic time in Arabian history when women could be out in public wearing less restrictive garments:

> *And abide still in your houses, and go not in public decked as in the day of your former ignorance...* (Q.33:33).

Women were respected more by the Arabs before Islam. They were called equals and companions, and treated as people with free choice. No one had the right to regard them as second class, slaves or animals. Just like men, their creative and influential role was evident everywhere. After Islam, their social status and influence decreased radically.[1]

The Gospel of the Son Jesus Christ is against:

- Women's immodesty before male relatives
  > *Women adorn themselves in modest apparel, with propriety and moderation ...* (1Timothy 2:9), *older women as mothers, younger as sisters, with all purity* (1Timothy 5:2).

- The discrimination to women
- The assertion of superiority of men over women
- The assertion of superiority of non-slaves over slaves
  > *There is neither Jew nor Greek, there is neither slave nor free, there is neither male nor female; for you are all one in Christ Jesus* (Galatians 3:28).

---

1   Read R. A. Nicholson, PP.87-90.

In contrast, Qur'anic faith and rule allow all the above immoralities and discriminations happen to women. Slavery is cherished in the Qur'an and non-Muslim girls and women are used as sex slaves.[1]Also, there is no protection for women in Islam; they are exposed to every kind of abuse on one hand, but on the other hand they are responsible for the temptation which afflicts men.[2]

The oppressive treatment of women by Islamic leaders can never be reconciled with the teaching of Jesus Christ. He calls such abuses the immorality of fleshly people. His goal is to free people from the immoral desires of flesh and establishing them in the kingdom of heaven. This freedom is provided through His death on the Cross. He frees men, women, children, slaves and masters from immorality through His atoning death and resurrection and gives them heavenly identity so that they see all equal in the eyes of God regardless of their race or gender.

The Leading Agent of Purification

The Gospel of Jesus Christ, unlike the Qur'an, teaches us that the salvation of individuals comes before their moral purification and perfection. A person is not able to represent the goodness of God unless transferred to that first state; that is, saved and reconciled with God. In other words, a person cannot be morally good until saved from evil and born into goodness. According to the Christian Gospel, a person cannot get rid of sexual immorality, impurity and debauchery, idolatry and witchcraft, hatred and discord, jealousy, fits of rage, selfish ambition, drunkenness, orgies, and the like until renewed by God and saved from the corrupted nature. In Christianity, God first changes the status of a person before extending the invitation to act righteously. The person must first be brought into a right situation or state in order to do right. However, in

---

1 Q. 4: 24-25;

2 Muhammad Sa'id Ramadan, *Al-Buti, Ela kul Fataten Tu'min be-Allah,* Mu'asat ar-Risalah, Beirut, 1987, English Edition, P.19, Commenting on Q.3:13).

Islam, it is the opposite. A sinful person is asked to do or be morally good before being enabled to be so.

Following rituals or enforcing a religious law by political forces cannot guarantee the moral purity of a person or a society. Political forces are not able to rescue a human soul from the effect of spiritual evil. An *inner* change is needed in order to give a person a fresh start. Therefore, moral purification is the *consequence* of salvation, which is the exodus from the power and effects of evil. God first saves and then He empowers people to be good and just in their relationships

This theological comparison between Islam and Christianity indicates that the Christian faith, not the Muslim faith, has the privilege of being the model for good morality on earth. We all know that issues of morality and immorality are the most important issues for life on earth. Immorality started on earth after Adam and Eve sinned against God, and has been a problem ever since. Therefore, immorality must be dealt with during life on earth.

There is another major difference between Islam and Christianity. Islam falls short of accepting God's own initiative for renewing the hearts of humankind. The fallen man's first need is to be unchained by God; that is, purified by God. This is what the Bible teaches. If a person's heart has not risen from its fallen state, the impure deeds of that impure heart cannot link to the pure, holy, just, caring and loving God. In other words, a heart must be renewed first in order to get the inspirations of God concerning good things. This means that God must be at work and in control of this great change:

> *When you were slaves of sin, you were free in regard to righteousness. What fruits did you have then in the things of which you are now ashamed? For the end of those things is death. But now having been set free from sin, and having become slaves of God, you have your fruit to holiness, and the end, everlasting life* (Romans 6:20-22).

It is apparent that many people in the Christian world have failed to surrender themselves to Jesus Christ even though they call themselves Christians. Immorality has spread among many who claim to live under the name of Christianity. For the Gospel of Jesus Christ, there is only one type of Christian in the world, only those who are saved to serve as Christ did. Christians are challenged throughout the Gospel to attain this.

Muslims, therefore, must not take the immorality of so-called Christian societies as a sign of the Christian faith having shortcomings. It would be a great help for Muslims in removing their misconceptions, if they would refer to the Gospel of Jesus Christ and compare it with their own religious scriptures. The central task of Jesus' words is to establish our hearts and minds on higher ground so that we can understand God's standard and live it.[1] Those who believe in Jesus are empowered to live with heightened morality in order to grow continually, as the Apostle Paul says; "… *inwardly we are being renewed day by day.*" (2 Corinthians. 4:16). The resulting renewal is lived out in loving and just relationships.

---

1 R. Zacharias, P.36.

5

The Teaching of Muhammad

God Is Unknowable?

God Is Unique?

Teaching Concerning Prophets

What Does It Mean To Be a Good Muslim?

Blind Obedience

Fighting Freedom

God Is Unknowable?

In Islam, the God of the universe stands outside of Muhammad's and his followers' understanding and consciousness as an unknowable and impersonal God. He does not have any personality in order to prove his existence to the personal humanity and build relationship with them.[1] The Qur'an says:

> He it is Who has sent down to thee the Book [Qur'an]: In it are verses basic or fundamental [of established meaning]; they are the foundation of the Book: others are allegorical. But those in whose hearts is perversity follow the part thereof that is allegorical, seeking discord, and searching for its hidden meanings, but **no one knows its hidden meanings except Allah**. And those who are firmly grounded in knowledge say: "We believe in the Book; the whole of it is f rom our Lord" and none will grasp the Message except men of understanding (Q.3:7, bold added).

Muhammad says through the Qur'an:

> If I [Muhammad] had knowledge of the unseen, I should have multiplied all good, and no evil should have touched me (Q.7:188)

So, Muhammad, who is the most favorite man of Allah, does not know Allah and understand his words. Muslims, in the same way, do not know the fundamental meaning of Qur'an's call and are unable to discern its central message or the real plan and purpose of Allah's guidance. Allah is absolutely without a person, non-revealing, invisible and therefore unknowable, but Muslims are still forced to follow Allah and his religion, Islam, without knowing him!

Islam's historical documents say also that Muhammad was not able to see Allah:

---

1   J. B. Taylor, P.14. & N.L. Geisler. & A. Saleeh, PP.262-3. & D. M. Lang, PP.9, 137. & K. Cragg, P.55.

Narrated Masruq: I said to Aisha, "O Mother! Did Prophet Muhammad see his Lord?" Aisha said, "What you have said makes my hair stand on end! Know that if somebody tells you one of the following three things, he is a liar: **Whoever tells you that Muhammad saw his Lord, is a liar."** *Then Aisha recited the Verse: "No vision can grasp Him, but His grasp is over all vision. He is the Most Courteous Well-Acquainted with all things."* (Q.6:103, bold added)

"It is not fitting for a human being that Allah should speak to him except by inspiration or from behind a veil." (Q.42:51, bold added)

Aisha further said, **"And whoever tells you that the Prophet knows what is going to happen tomorrow, is a liar."** *She then recited:* **"No soul can know what it will earn tomorrow."** (Q.31:34, bold added)

She added: "And whoever tells you that he concealed [some of Allah's orders], *is a liar." Then she recited: "O Apostle! Proclaim* [the Message] *which has been sent down to you from your Lord."* (5.67) *Aisha added. "But the Prophet saw Gabriel in his true form twice."*[1]

This is the main reason that the Muslim scholars adapted the Neo-Platonic philosophy and based their doctrine on it. The Neo-Platonic[2] concept of oneness views God as being in absolute unity in which there is no multiplicity of characteristics (personalities) at all and is, therefore, unknowable by personal beings. This explains why Muslims are unable to understand

---

1 Bukhari, Volume 6, Book 60, Hadith 378.

2 Neo-Platonism developed from the philosophy of Plato's *theory of forms,* which says humankind's knowledge comes from recognising the essential form of a thing, rather than from observing its many incidental qualities. The Neo-Platonists carried the theory a step further, by saying that there is single highest form, *The One* that is incomprehensible. It is a mistake even to say that The One *"is,"* because the one is beyond being (Neo-Platonism, *The World Book Encyclopaedia*).

the Trinity (the three personalities) of the One God. They have been taught that God is impersonal or non-revealing; he does not have any personality in order to reveal and relate himself personally to them as personal beings. That is why he cannot be present to love the fallen man and save him. However, a question can be raised here: If Allah does not have any personality and cannot be present by any personality, where does he get his forceful personality to require people to leave their religions and blindly follow him? The answer to this question will lead you to understand that Islam is a man-made religion and it cannot be from the real and personal God. A personal man, Muhammad, confuses himself (like many others do) and his followers between his personality and impersonality of Allah. Eventually, his attitudes become the attitudes of Allah who is impersonal and cannot have any personal attitude!

Muhammad's own experience when he was receiving the first message of Islam from the angel Gabriel conveys his understanding of God. At the very beginning, the foundation of Islam was based on "blind" obedience that did not require any knowledge about, or understanding of the message. Gabriel forced him to simply recite words from his mouth that were incomprehensible to him. He stood against the force with all his strength. However, he could not stand the unbearable pressure, gave up trying to resist and surrendered himself to the will of unknowable Allah. It is believed that Allah armed Gabriel on one hand with the Qur'an, and on the other with sufficient force to win the blind obedience of Muhammad. This became the process used for Islam's expansion ever since the rise of Islam as a state religion.

The way in which Muhammad received the Qur'an through an angel and not through Allah himself, unavoidably encourages Muslims to link their theology to the Neo-Platonic ideas about the invisibility and unknowability of God. How could an unknowable God, who did not expect Muhammad to comprehend him, expect Muslim scholars to comprehend him? So this gives Muslim scholars good reason to assert the unknowability of God, as God chose not to appear to Muhammad directly and make himself known to him.

There are scientific problems in Islamic philosophy. From Muhammad's experience with the angel Gabriel, we understand that Gabriel is also personal; otherwise, he wouldn't be able to reveal himself to Muhammad. How then could the impersonal Allah relate or reveal himself to the personal Gabriel, asking him to take his personal message (Qur'an) to Muhammad? An impersonal god cannot relate to any personal being (neither man nor angel) and cannot have any personal message. If this is the case, how then can the Qur'an be taken as the personal words of the impersonal Allah who is absolutely away from every personality and cannot make any personal word? If Allah cannot make any word, he, therefore, cannot be The Word himself. In other words, if God is the Word, and if Allah is not the Word, he therefore is not God.

The unknowability of God in Islam has created a chaotic doctrine in Islam. It opposes Muhammad's own claim concerning the superiority of Islam to the Jewish and Christian religions. In Judaism and Christianity God personally showed Himself to the prophets and his followers. This is what the Qur'an also confirms (Q.4:164). Why would God choose direct revelation of Himself in a so-called "less important" religion (Muslims view Christianity and Judaism lesser than Islam) but indirect revelation in Islam, a so-called superior and complete religion? Surely a complete religion necessitates a full and complete revelation? Indeed, a complete religion must remove all barriers and reveal God to His people, reconciling them to Him.

Also, the "unknowable" doctrine of Islam stands in opposition to the teaching of the Qur'an about God's relationship with humankind. This teaching includes the episode when God formed man from the dust by "*his hands*" and "*breathed*" into the dust and man became alive:

> ...*Lord said to the angel, "I am about to make man of clay, And when I have formed him and breathed my spirit into him, then worshipping fall down before him...whom my hands have made"* (Q.38:71,72,75).

The intimate relationship between God and Adam at the time of creation as also described by the Qur'an does not fit with Islamic doctrine of the absolutist, impersonal and unknowable essence of God. How can we say that God touched Adam and breathed His spirit into him, dealing personally with him, and yet at the same time assert that God was an impersonal stranger to Adam? The above qur'anic verses bring forth the meaning that Adam was not soulless dust, but was someone who received a personality from his Creator, saw his Creator and was enabled to carry the witness of Him. It was the personal inspirations of the personal God in Adam that made Adam a living creature and, therefore, a living messenger to his offspring. The creation proves that God is a personal God who relates Himself to His creatures through His personalities.

The nature of the work of creation implies a tight connection between the essence of God, His works and His created man and woman. They understood that God created them. God desired to create them. He translated His desire into action in order to have fellowship with them. He wanted to treasure them and to enjoy His mutual relationship with them. As a result, they were able to see who God was and the purpose of God in creation. There was not any kind of veil between God and the mind and heart of humankind at the time of creation. There was nothing causing a lack of understanding about God.

This changed when Adam sinned against God leading to the issue of a veil or separation between God and humankind. Such a separation became a serious threat for life on earth. After Adam sinned against God, God took the initiative to unveil the heart and mind of Adam. He helped him to tap into his God-given understanding and capacity for remembering the beauty of God's presence with Him before sin entered the world.

God created humankind with the ability to understand and He has continued His work of opening the heart and mind of humankind toward understanding. He has created people in such a way that they might understand Him. After Adam's fall, the work of God was always to unveil the mind and heart of each individual in order to enable each one to grasp and describe the fruitfulness and the beauty of His presence among them:

> *O LORD, you are my God; I will exalt you and praise your name, for in perfect faithfulness you have done marvelous things,…You have been a refuge for the poor, and refuge for the needy in his distress, a shelter from the storm and a shade from the heat…. The sovereign LORD will wipe away the tears from all faces;… In that day they will say, "Surely this is our God; we trusted in him, and he saved us…let us rejoice and be glad in his salvation"* (Isaiah 25:1,4,8,9).

God in Christ revealed Himself to the world in order to open the minds and the hearts of the lost world and in this way to take them back to His kingdom. The Son Jesus Christ came down from heaven to remove the veil, to free the world and to return it to its first state of freedom. (See 2 Corinthians 3:12-18).

God is a revealing God, and He reveals Himself with all His personalities and characteristics, but only for those who desire to see Him and be freed from their veils through their faith in the Son Jesus Christ.

It will be impossible for a person to be a messenger of God's words without experiencing His personal presence and life-changing works. The knowledge of God without the experience of God's presence is worth nothing. The godly life makes sense only when God is personally present in our hearts, thoughts, words and deeds.

One reason that Islam offers no assurance of salvation is because it rejects the possibility of its followers experiencing God during life on earth. That is why it has become so difficult for Muslims to comprehend the new life in Christianity. In Islam many attractive and elegant words were preserved carefully, sensitively, lovingly and sacrificially from generation to generation. They were influential and inseparable parts of the culture, but still worthless for experiential salvation. The words of Islam can be memorized and kept in the mind, loved in the heart, but only as the words of a tradition or of a law. Muslims really fell in love with their religion and even put their lives on the line for their beliefs, yet their beliefs were unable to save their souls. Their beliefs are not able to incarnate God in their hearts. They are unable, therefore, to leave a clear confession proclaiming that the job was completed, that they have reached their goals and are united with God. They have no assurance that their bondage to sin, Satan and hell was abolished and that God is with and in them forever (Immanuel).

If the doctrine of Islam, which testifies to the impersonality and unknowability of God, was true, then the Garden of Eden would have allowed for no relationship between God and Adam and Eve. Accordingly, rebellion and sin would not make sense, as there would have been no intimate relationship between God and humankind that could be broken. Therefore, there would be no need for humankind to repent and to long for fellowship with God. Likewise, there would be no need for God to acknowledge humankind's confession. The paradise that Islam looks forward to after death would not include an intimate and personal relationship between God and humankind. It is a garden with flowing streams, with beautiful greenery, fruits and maidens for men (Q.2:25; Q.52:22-23; 44:51-55). It is therefore hardly attractive to the heart that seeks after God and asks for his protection. If the living spirit of a human being, given to that person by the living Spirit of God, cannot know the Creator, then none of these concepts make sense: belief, unbelief, rebellion, repentance, submission, godly living, judgment, paradise, acceptance or rejection, because the goal and joy of knowing God personally is unreachable. Therefore, any doctrinal interest in Islam fails to be convincing and furthermore, fails to meet the hunger and thirst of humankind for the Creator. People taking shelter in God is something that does not make any sense to a Muslim..

It is instructive to understand that a Muslim introduces himself as a *Khalifatallah* (vicegerent, i.e., God's representative). He fails to recognize that this isn't supported by Islamic doctrine of the impersonality and unknowability of his god. God's reign cannot be manifested by Muslim rulers when He is regarded as an inaccessible god. If Allah is not accessible, he cannot sit upon any human throne and rule with appointed vicegerents (See Q.2:31). Accordingly, none of the Islamic governments can call themselves the agents of Allah. Who can claim to be the ruler for God when he is not able to sense the qualities of God's ruling Spirit?

If God is not understandable, then the Islamic mission of wanting to rule the world on behalf of Allah becomes invalid according to the doctrine of Islam. Even when Muhammad presents himself as the prophet of God, this does not fit with the Islamic doctrine of impersonality of God that no one can submit to God (a complete contradiction to the meaning of Islam which is "submission") and walk closely in relationship with Him. Furthermore, the Qur'an, which calls itself a guide for humankind to know God, cannot make sense since God is unknowable in Islam. For example, the Qur'an introduces God as the compassionate and merciful God at the beginning of all its chapters, but one. If God is impersonal and unknowable, then what does compassion or mercy mean and how are they understood and received personally?

Muslim scholars need to acknowledge these inconsistencies. The Qur'an contradicts itself in many places. On one hand, it says that no one is able to understand Allah, but on the other hand it asks Muslims to understand. What does it mean, in the following Qur'anic verses, when it speaks of 'understanding'?

> *An Arabic Koran have we sent it down, that ye might understand it* (Q.12:2).

> *We have made it an Arabic Koran that ye may understand.* (Q.43:3).

> *We have created man from the union of the sexes that we might prove him; and hearing, seeing, have we made him* (Q.76:2).

If God is understandable, He therefore must be personal. If He is personal, He therefore must love and save you personally. Why then did Muhammad die with uncertainty and why do Muslims die without salvation?

Paul, the apostle of Christ, has written eye-opening words on how one person can understand God:

> *For what man knows the things of a man except the spirit of the man which is in him? Even so no one knows the things of God except the Spirit of God. Now we have received, not the spirit of the world, but the Sprit who is from God, that we might know the things that have been freely given to us by God. These things we also speak, not in words which man's wisdom teaches but which the Holy Spirit teaches, comparing spiritual things with spiritual. But the natural man does not receive the things of the Spirit of God, for they are foolishness to him; nor can he know them, because they are spiritually discerned. But he who is spiritual judges all things, yet he himself is rightly judged by no one. For who has known the mind of the LORD that he may instruct Him? But we have the mind of Christ* (1 Corinthians 2:11-16).

Jesus Christ revealed Himself in order to establish the Spirit of God in people's heart and make God known to them, so that they could see the glory of God, fall in love with Him and submit themselves to Him. He said:

Father... I have manifested Your name to the men whom You have given Me out of the world ... For I have given to them the words which You have given Me; and they have received them, and have known surely that I came forth from You: and they have believed that You sent Me (John 17:1, 6, 8).

God Is Unique?

Unique, but not in Creation

It is curious to note that the Qur'an itself, although it defends the unity of Allah and attributes the work of creation to him alone (cf. Q.2:255; 6:101; 13:16; 112:1-4), seems indecisive in rejecting the idea of "*other creators*";

> *Blessed therefore be Allah, the most excellent of Makers.* (Q.23:14).

The word for *Makers* in the above verse is *Khalighein* in Arabic which means *Creators*. This can be taken to mean that although Allah is not the creator of all creatures, he is the best creator among the multiple creators. It could be for the same reason that in many places in the Qur'an, Allah is referred to in plural form, by the pronoun "we" rather than the singular "I". Muhammad borrowed this belief from pagans. For Pagans, Allah was the most excellent god and creator among all other gods in Mecca.

This plurality, no matter for whatever reason that is used in the Qur'an, cannot rest easily with Islam's practice of rigid and inflexible monotheism. In Islam, plurality of any kind-- whether a sign of respect and power or a word for describing God's personalities--brings the absolute unity of Allah under question. He is an impersonal god and without a nature, who does not have any personality to be known and compared with others. [1]

---

1 N.L. Geisler & A. Saleeh, P.135.

Though many Muslims scholars have written that Allah is absolutely unique in his creation, in his revelation and in anything he wills and does, these sayings are all against the impersonal and unknowable doctrine of Islam about Allah. He cannot reveal himself in order to prove that he is unique in his wills, words and actions. It is not possible to say that there are multiple personalities in impersonal Allah since impersonality verses personality.

Unique, but not in Revelation

The second reason that Allah cannot be called unique is because of his revelation, the Qur'an. As the evidence shows, the overall theology of the Qur'an is brought under question by its many paradoxical verses:

Contradictions	
Say: Allah is alone … (Q.112).	Allah is the most excellent of Creators (Q.23:14).

Why other "Creators", if Allah is absolutely alone?

Contradictions	
And [Jesus] shall be a Sign [for the coming of] the Hour [of Judgment]: therefore have no doubt about the [Hour], but follow ye Me: this is a Straight Way (Q.43:61).	Muhammad is …the Apostle of Allah, and the Seal of the Prophets: and Allah has full knowledge of all things (Q.33:40).

If Muhammad is the seal of prophets and came to perfect the work of all previous prophets, why is Jesus then predicted to come back and perfect the job?

Contradictions	
O children of Adam let not Satan bring you into trouble, as he drove forth your parents from the Garden (Q.7:27).	For him whom Allah leads astray, you [Muhammad] shall by no means find a pathway (Q.4:88).

If Allah is not happy with the Satan's troubles, why is he himself bringing people into the same troubles?

Contradictions	
Allah has not placed two hearts in any man's body (Q.32:4).	Allah has fashioned the soul with debauchery and righteousness (Q.91:8).

If Allah has fashioned the soul with dualism, his created heart also will be dualistic!

Contradictions	
We granted not to any man before thee permanent life [here]: if then thou shouldst die, would they live permanently? Every soul shall have a taste of death: and We test you by evil and by good by way of trial. to Us must ye return (Q.21:34-35).	That they said (in boast), "We killed Christ Jesus the son of Mary, the Apostle of Allah"; but they killed him not, nor crucified him,... Allah raised him up unto Himself; and Allah is Exalted in Power, Wise (Q.4:157-158).

On one hand, Allah says that before Muhammad no one had a permanent life, but on the other hand he says that Jesus did not die but was raised to heaven and has a permanent life according to the Qur'an. He said that every man should die, why then did Jesus not die since he was called a man in the Qur'an? Does this mean that Jesus was not a man, or if he was,

was his manhood different and superior to the manhood of Muhammad who died?

Again as we have seen earlier, the various contradicting early manuscripts of the Qur'an is also another problem that makes the absolute unity of Allah impossible. Among the early manuscripts of the Qur'an, there was no absolute unity that was evident. Therefore, this lack of unity among the manuscripts proves that the source of this revelation was not unique. Muslims believe that nobody can change the words of Allah. Therefore, the changes that were evident among the eight different Qur'ans could not be from man but from Allah. Therefore, if Allah's words contradict one another, he cannot be unique.

Among eight Qur'ans, Muhammad's successor, Othman, selected one Qur'an as the true one and burned all others. His choice cannot be true according to Islam's absolutist philosophy. No humankind, including a prophet, is able with his limited knowledge to discern the absolute revelation from a group of revelations. Islamic traditions say to us that even Muhammad, as the beloved of Allah, had trouble distinguishing the right from the wrong verses. He allowed all versions to be used, therefore, how could Othman be able to discover the true revelations?

Furthermore, the Qur'an, Muhammad's own successors and early Islamic theologians all attributed a few words of idol exaltation to Muhammad and asserted that he used these words some times in his prophetic ministry. As Muslims believe, idol worshiping is against the nature of Allah and belongs to Satan. Muslims also believe that the Qur'an was written by Allah in eternity. This shows that the idol exaltation in the Qur'an was an eternal issue in Islam that was started by Allah. How could Allah be called unique, if he himself has ordained the exaltation of idols and Satan? This also comes in sharp contradiction to the Qur'an's own saying about the complete and enduring faithfulness of the Jewish messengers, whereby they worshipped the only existing God and rejected idol exaltation:

> *And question thou our apostles whom We sent before thee; did We appoint any deities other than (Allah) Most Gracious, to be worshipped?* (Q.43:45).

Unique, but not in Worshipping

Muhammad stood in favor of maintaining the practices and desires of pagan converts to Islam, when he authenticated the pilgrimage to Mecca and the custom of bowing before a black stone and kissing it, all of which belonged to pre-Islamic idolatrous rituals (Q.2:158; 22:26-27). Worshipping and kissing a stone appear to be idolatrous and lawless acts and therefore oppose the monotheistic view of God presented in Islamic theology.

How do these actions carried out by Muhammad come to be forbidden for everyone else, but remain as acceptable for the prophet of Islam? Why did Muhammad slaughter pagans for the sake of their rituals which he made his own later? He blamed the people of the Book (Christians and Jews) for going beyond the truth and yet he was not able to avoid this himself:

> *O ye people of the Book! Overstep not bounds in your religion; and of God speak only truth...* (Q.4:171).

How can a system of thought criticize others for their sins, while it has condoned the same sins in its sacred writings? Why do Muslim leaders and writers pay no attention to their own sin recorded in their holy book but still condemn others and very often give formal orders to kill others by accusing them of the same sin?

The main reason for this problem is in the nature of Islam. Islam has not allowed itself to be scrutinized by the most valuable source of advice--namely self-criticism regarding one's approach to others.

Conversely, Jesus Christ strongly urges self-examination before judgment of others. Truly, the name "Jesus" or "The Son" is the only way that all the nations of the world can be rightly united to each other, because His is the way of love. This unity cannot be achieved unless people follow the humble steps and advice of Jesus Christ. It is here again that the Qur'an and the Bible differ from each other sharply when Jesus says:

> *"How can you say to your brother, 'Let me remove the speck from of your eye,' and look, a plank is in your own eye? Hypocrite! First remove the plank from your own eye, and then you will see clearly to remove the speck from your brother's eye"* (Matthew 7:4,5).

Teaching Concerning Prophets

Contrary to Muhammad, the prophets of the Bible gave up their worldly fame to take shelter in the eternal glory of the coming Son, Jesus Christ. Moses sacrificed his political fame for faith in the coming promise. He resigned from the kingdom of Egypt just for the sake of the Son Jesus Christ, the eternal Redeemer (Hebrews 11:26).

Muhammad also, like all the prophets of the Bible, had a choice in front of him. He had to choose between *the Son Jesus Christ* (he accepted Jesus Christ as the Son of God early on in Mecca) *or the new political power, fame and pleasure* he had established in the world (in Medina). The Son of the Bible, who came to establish the eternal kingdom among the nations of the world, was left outside the heart of Islam. Instead, He was introduced as the one who tried his best to establish an earthly kingdom, but failed to do so. Muhammad, as the seal of the prophets, took over the task of completing an earthly kingdom and launched the march from Medina. His Islamic belief system was heading along a path that was not in line with the biblical path.

The biblical path is the path of knowledge and understanding. Those who adhere to the biblical teaching have the right to weigh the authenticity of the words they hear from any who claim to be a prophet. God said to Moses:

> *Whoever will not hear My words, which He speaks in My name, I will require it of him. The prophet who presumes to speak a word in My name, which I have not commanded him to speak, or who speaks in the name of other gods, that prophet shall die* (Deuteronomy 18:19-20).

In biblical faith, it was not the people who did not listen to the messages of God that ought to be put to death immediately. Rather, the one who called himself a prophet and misled people to accept his words as God's words ought to be put to death. Furthermore, God spoke through Moses to the people:

> *And if you say in your heart, 'How shall we know the word which the LORD has not spoken? When a prophet speaks in the name of the LORD, if the things does not happen or come to pass, that is the thing which the LORD has not spoken; the prophet has spoken it presumptuously; you shall not be afraid of him* (Deuteronomy 18:21-22).

If these words of Moses are compared with what the Qur'an says about Muslims' responsibilities toward Muhammad, it becomes crystal clear that the two paths are going in opposite directions:

> *Those who deny Allah and His apostles, and* [those who] *wish to separate Allah from His apostles, saying: "We believe in some but reject others": And* [those who] *wish to take a course midway,--They are in truth* [equally] *unbelievers; and we have prepared for unbelievers a humiliating punishment. To those who believe in Allah and His apostles and make no distinction between any of the apostles, we shall soon give their* [due] *rewards: for Allah is Oft-forgiving, Most Merciful* (Q.4:150-152).

> *It is not fitting for a Believer, man or woman, when a matter has been decided by Allah and His Apostle to have any option*

about their decision: if any one disobeys Allah and His Apostle, he is indeed on a clearly wrong Path (Q.33:36).

Remember thy Lord inspired the angels [with the message]: *"I am with you: give firmness to the Believers: I will instil terror into the hearts of the Unbelievers: smite ye above their necks and smite all their finger-tips off them." This because they contended against Allah and His Apostle: If any contend against Allah and His Apostle, Allah is strict in punishment* (Q.8:12-13).

Biblical Path	*Qur'anic Path*
people have a choice	people have no choice
people are not slaughtered because of their different faith	people are slaughtered because of their different faith
people have a right to test whatever they hear	people have no right to test whatever they hear
people have a right to inquire about the prophet's words and deeds	people have no right to question the prophet at all
a prophet is accountable to individuals for his words and deeds, because every individual is called to look after the society both spiritually and physically	a prophet is not accountable to the society because the ultimate authority is in his hands. Individuals must obey him
people worship God and know Him	people worship God without knowing him

In the Bible, prophets do not hold themselves above others because of their positions. They are simply the vessels of God to convey His words to people. They humble themselves and confess that there is not even one person on the earth who can be relied on as a standard of righteousness. Everybody must keep his/her eyes toward heaven where their Savior comes from:

> *We are all like an unclean thing, and all our righteousnesses are like filthy rags; we all fade as leaf, and our iniquities, like the wind, have taken us away* (Isaiah 64:6).

> *There is none righteous, no, not one* (Romans 3:10; Psalms 14:1-3).

> *Our God whom we serve is able to deliver us ....* (Daniel 3:17), *The Mighty One will save* (Zephaniah 3:17).

> *For God did not send his Son into the world to condemn the world, but that the world through Him might be saved* (John 3:17).

The Bible, unlike the Qur'an, is not to condemn those who are against God or prophets, but to save them through loving, kind and sacrificial approaches. God knows that man is fallen and he will not be able to please Him if he is not saved and made righteous. For this reason, He comes and saves them like a loving parent in order to prepare the ground for them to act righteous.

The revelations in the Bible help all groups of people to humble themselves in the presence of God and seek righteousness only from Him. According to the Bible, every person, including prophets, are alike; they were born from sinful parents and are in need of salvation from God. The following verses of the Bible show the crying out of the king and prophet, David, who declares the unworthiness of his deeds and position before God as he begs for immediate salvation;

> *Wash me thoroughly from my iniquity, and cleanse me from sin. For I acknowledge my transgressions, and my sin is always before me. Against You, You only, have I sinned, and done this evil in Your sight ... Create in me a clean heart, O God, and renew a steadfast spirit within me* (Psalms 51:2-4,10).

It is foolish to rely on someone, who himself, like everyone else on the earth, is in desperate need of salvation from God. It is even more foolish to take the whole life and teaching of such a person as an absolute authority for how to live one's life on earth and the life after. That is why the Bible calls upon people to not blindly obey such invitations, but to make sure whether they are right or wrong. In the Bible, every invitation is first directed to the minds and hearts of people for evaluation and examination so that they can distinguish between right and wrong and choose the channel that leads to the true path. That channel is the true God. The Bible curses those who rely on even prophets as mediators for salvation. Trust must be placed only in God who is the Savior of all. Even prophets sin and fall, but God is holy and trustworthy:

> *Then the LORD said to me: "Even if Moses and Samuel stood before Me, My mind would not be favorable toward this people* (Jeremiah 15:1).

> *"...when a land sins against Me ... even though Noah, Daniel, and Job were in it, as I live," Says the Lord God, "they would deliver neither son nor daughter; they would deliver only themselves by their righteousness."* (Ezekiel 14:13, 20).

> *Thus says the LORD: "Cursed is the man who trusts in man, and makes flesh his strength...."* (Jeremiah 17:5).

In biblical faith, the mediator cannot be one who is from the earth but must be someone who is in and from heaven (paradise). The job of the earthly prophet is to preach repentance and to beg for the intercessory work of the One who is in and from heaven. The One in and from heaven is a stranger to sin, and is in no need of repentance. That is why even the righteous ones of the earth are not able to intercede for the lives of others before God. This is because their own righteousness is the result of God's intercessory grace toward them after they repented and asked God to establish them in His kingdom. The mediator, therefore, must be someone who is totally on God's side and has never sinned against God and people. This biblical testimony goes against the words of the Qur'an that calls people to rely on Muhammad and on whatever he said or did. According to the Qur'an, Muhammad was a sinful man and thus in desperate need of a mediator for salvation:

> *And the burdened soul shall not bear the burden of another: and if the heavy laden soul cry out for its burden to be carried, yet shall not aught of it be carried, even by the near of kin!...* (Q.35:18).

> *[S]eek pardon for thy* [Muhammad] *fault...*(Q.40:55; cf. 47:19; 48:2).

Muhammad himself was a sinner (unrighteous in the presence of God), as he himself confessed that he was not sure of his future life (Q.46:9). His followers were also unsaved like him and were sinners and unrighteous in the same way. So, there is no difference between Muhammad and a sinner. Sadly, Muhammad was not able to see his sin and short-comings and he instructed cutting the fingertips and heads off of those who acted towards him against his desires. Why would an unrighteous person cut off the fingers and head of another for the same unrighteousness he himself is struggling with?

What Does It Mean to Be a Good Muslim?

The Qur'an says those Muslims who take part in the jihad for killing the non-Muslims are set apart in the eyes of Allah compared with those who do not join the jihad. Fighters are considered superior to others:

> *War is prescribed to you: but from this you are averse....* (Q.2:216).

> *Those believers who sit at home free from trouble, and those who do valiantly in the cause of God with their substance and their persons, shall not be treated alike. God hath assigned to those who contend earnestly with their persons and with their substance, a rank above those who sit at home. Goodly promises hath He made to all. But God has assigned to the*

strenuous a rich recompense, above those who sit still at home (Q.4: 95).

They who were left at home were delighted to stay behind God's Apostle, and were averse from contending with their riches and their persons for the cause of God, and said, "March not out in the heat." SAY: "A fiercer heat will be the fire of Hell." Would that they understood this (Q.9:81).

Therefore, the invasion of non-Muslims became the focal point of the faith of every true Muslim. Accordingly, invasions became the major tool for the spread of Islam and, in fact, spreading Islam became the main reason for going to war. In this way, Islam became the official religion of Arabia bringing every aspect of the life of the people under its control. Therefore, the teachings and acts of Muhammad and his successors caused Muslims, down through the centuries, to feel they had an obligation to wage battles and to inflict violence against non-Muslims.

To the fundamentalist Muslim, the population of the world is divided into two groups, Muslims (clean) and non-Muslims (unclean). According to the Qur'an, there can be no peace between these two groups. The Qur'an orders Muslims to kill those who worship other gods and who do not believe in Islam, until all the earth becomes subjected to the rule of Islam:

And when the sacred months are passed, kill those who join other gods with God wherever ye shall find them; and seize them, besiege them, and lay wait for them with every kind of ambush: but if they shall convert, and observe prayer, and pay the obligatory alms, then let them go their way, for God is Gracious, Merciful (Q.9:5)

When you encounter the infidels, strike off their heads till ye have make a great slaughter among them, and of the rest make fast the fetters. And afterwards let there either be free dismissals or ransomings, till the war hath laid down its burdens. Thus do. Were such the pleasure of God, he could himself take vengeance upon them: but He would rather prove the one of you by the other. And whoso fight for the cause of God, their works he will not suffer to miscarry (Q.47:4).

Say to the infidels; If they desist from their unbelief, what is now past shall be forgiven them; but if they return to it, they have already before them the doom of the ancients! Fight then against them till strife be at an end, and the religion be all of it God's. If they desist, verily God beholdeth what they do (Q.8:38-39).

And remember when God promised you [Muslims] *that one of the two troops should fall to you, and ye desired that they who had no arms should fall to you: but God purposed to prove true the truth of his words, and to cut off the uttermost part of the infidels* (Q.8:7).

However, a way out was provided for those Jews and Christians who, in a sense, did not want to be killed by Muslims. Their obligation to the Muslims was that they had to abide by the Islamic laws and pay a yearly amount, or jizya, to the Islamic ruler in order to live:

Make war upon such of those to whom the Scripture have been given as believe not in God, or in the last day, and who forbid not that which God and His Apostle have forbidden, and who profess not the profession of the truth, until they pay tribute out of hand, and they be humbled (Q.9: 29).

The issue of paying jizya was not followed as prescribed in the Qur'an all of the time. Its legitimacy has depended very much on the various circumstances in Islamic societies. Some have favored the use of pressure, persecution, terror and the like rather than getting tribute. Some favored less pressure and therefore preferred tribute accomplished by humiliation; *they be humbled* (Q.9: 29), Qur'an says. Some others preferred to ignore both.

The instructions of the Qur'an concerning the yearly tribute and the humiliation are to put pressures on the People of the

Book (Christians, Jews, Sabeites (or Sabians) and Zoroastrians) and force them to free themselves from the law of *Dhimmitude*[1] and embrace Islam.

The Qur'an says:

> ... *If only the People of the Book had faith, it were best for them: among them are some who have faith, but most of them are perverted transgressors. ... Shame is pitched over them* [like a tent] *wherever they are found, except when under a covenant* [of protection] *from Allah and from men; they draw on themselves wrath from Allah, and pitched over them is* [the tent of] *destitution. This because they rejected the Signs of Allah, and slew the prophets in defiance of right; this because they rebelled and transgressed beyond bounds* (Q.3:110, 112).

What are the distinguishing principles for humiliating the People of the Book?

- They have to submit to Islamic law and pay yearly life money, or jizya, if they want to stay alive. They are enemies; enemies pay in return for protection, peace or reconciliation.
- They have to recognize the ownership of Islam over their lands (read Q.33:27).
- They have to dress poorly and use a different dress code or use colored patches in order to be distinguished from Muslims.
- They are not greeted by Muslims.
- They must keep to the side of the road when a Muslim walks in that road.
- They may not build higher than or as high as the Muslims' buildings.

---

1 *Dhimmitude* is a distinguishing principle in Islamic law for the treatment of conquered peoples who are called the People of the Book. They need to pay yearly in order to spare their lives and be humiliated in order to embrace Islam.

- They are forbidden to build new worship places or to repair damaged ones.
- They are forbidden to hinder a fellow person to embrace Islam.
- They do not have right to defend themselves if attacked.[1]

Furthermore, the jizya is collected via very humiliating rituals in a public place. The People of the Book are forced to stay in the lowest and dirtiest place. The Muslim officials, who represent the Islamic law, stand in a higher and clean place near them and ask for money while humiliating them with words or actions.[2] They do this in order to please Allah:

> *Those who resist Allah and His Apostle will be among those most humiliated. Allah has decreed: "It is I and My apostles who must prevail": For Allah is One full of strength, able to enforce His Will* (Q.58:20-21).

A true Muslim is always called to stay faithful to the teaching of the Qur'an and Muhammad, humiliating and fighting (jihad against) non-Muslims for the cause of Allah and spreading Islam. Even many nominal Muslims, consciously or unconsciously, are indirectly involved in the jihad against non-Muslims through their religious payments. The large amount of money that the religious leaders collect from Muslim communities is invested for the raising up of true Muslims who can follow the footsteps of Muhammad and humiliate the People of the Book or fight them. The giving of money is unavoidable for the majority of nominal Muslims. This is not solely because of the love they hold toward Islam, but because of the fear of evil spirits and the battles that are common in Islamic culture. Generally, people vow to pay to a mosque or to a saint's tomb. The giving is seen

---

1 Al-Mawardi, *The Laws of Islamic Governance*, 1058, PP. 60; 77-78; 200-201. & Reliance of the Traveller, PP.607-608.

2 Many examples of humiliations can be found in a book by Bat Ye'Or, The Dhimmi: Jews and Christians under Islam, USA: Madison, Fairleigh Dickinson, 1985.

as part of their religious duty or obligation--a good deed that might bring comfort to its giver or might increase the chance of entry into any desired situation, including paradise.

Muslims are called to safeguard their own life according to Islamic values and to try in any possible way to spread Islam among non-Islamic people.

Blind Obedience

Muhammad called Islam the last and most prefect religion in the world, but he did not believe in people's capability for evaluating his claim through a fundamental comparison with other beliefs.

When we call a religion the best and most complete of all, this means it has raised the certainty about a human being's salvation to the highest level in comparison to all other religions. It means that this religion has an attractive plan for reconciling humankind to God. But how can this be determined without searching among the various religions for truth? Do Muslims hold this view? If so they would be interested in knowing and understanding which is superior. They would want to find the religion that teaches genuine salvation, and would want to avoid the ones that are hopeless and provides no certainty of salvation.

A true religion encourages its followers to carefully consider all things and choose the best with a free will. God has not created us to blindly accept or follow His ideas and thoughts even though in His sovereignty over all things He could do so. Instead, He encourages understanding and acceptance that is based on weighing the evidence, because knowledge and understanding are part of His nature:

> ...*the Lord is a God who knows, and by him deeds are weighed* (1 Samuel 2: 3).

God has created and called us to be in His likeness. He has enabled us to consider His thoughts, words and deeds with open minds and make them the basis of our own beliefs. The characteristics of belief in the Bible are having knowledge, understanding and choosing the best of all based on testing:

> *But a prophet who presumes to speak in my [God] name anything I have not commanded him to say, or a prophet who speaks in the name of other gods, must be put to death. You may say to yourselves, "How can we know when a message has not been spoken by the LORD?" If what a prophet proclaims in the name of the LORD does not take place or come true, that is a message the LORD has not spoken. That prophet has spoken presumptuously. Do not be afraid of him* (Deuteronomy 18:20-22).

> *"Come now, let us reason together," says the LORD* (Isaiah 1:18).

> *…they [people] may see and know, and consider and understand,… "Present your case," says the LORD. "Bring forth your strong reasons," says the King of Jacob* (Isaiah 41:20-21).

> *Saying, 'Peace, peace!' when there is no peace* (Jeremiah 8:11b).

> *"And you shall know the truth, and the truth shall make you free"* (John 8:32).

> *Let two or three prophets speak, and let the others judge* (1 Corinthians 14:29).

> *Test all things; hold fast what is good* (1 Thessalonians 5:21).

> *Beloved, do not believe every spirit, but test the spirits, whether they are of God; because many false prophets have gone out into the world. By this you know the Spirit of God …* (1 John 4:1-2).

Through research, knowledge and weighing different words and beliefs, we will be able to find for ourselves the true words of the true God, and then live them out as our own. However, if there is no knowledge of the beliefs and values of others and consequently no ability to compare them with one's own beliefs and values, then why should one call himself and his religion superior to others? If anyone knows the truth, that truth can set him or her free, but the truth cannot be found by blindly following or obeying the wrong guides who have never made a proper comparison.

There are verses in the Qur'an that encourage a search for greater knowledge about other beliefs in order to discover the best. Unfortunately, neither Muhammad nor his followers applied this in their lives and they have just remained in words. This is because Islam is an authoritarian religion; authoritarians also speak good words, not for practicing them but for show:

> *For thy Lord is the most Beneficent, Who hath taught the use of pen; Hath taught Man that which he knoweth not* (Q.96:3-5).

> *On Earth are signs for men of firm belief, And also in your own selves: Will you not then behold them* (Q.51:20-21)?

> *And the blind and the seeing are not alike; neither darkness and light; nor the shade and hot wind* (Q.35:19).

This raises serious questions about the meaning of the word "faith" in Islam. "Faith" implies the capability of every Muslim to use his intelligence in order to see whether or not the words of Allah are practical.[1] Sadly, Muslims are forbidden to do so as they do not have any write to seek causes of dispute in the Qur'an or speak above the words of Muhammad.[2]

All religions, in one way or another, call upon their followers to put their faith into action. What is crucial, however, is to use our minds to understand the religions in the context of life in the world. God's Word must address itself to our minds so that we can use our intelligence to distinguish true from

---

1 W. C. Chittick, *Sufism*, USA: Oneworld Pub., 2000, P.6.

2 Q.2:176; 33:36.

false. Therefore, knowledge is the inseparable part of faith. Knowledge provides a place of confidence for faith to step into. Confidence, of course, is the result of a mindful search that results in a positive experience of reasoning. If someone decides to place confidence in God, it means that person has first examined the Word of God with the mind and heart and has discovered its relevancy to all dimensions of life. These are sadly what missing in Islam and Muslims' lives.

Fighting Freedom

The writings of the Qur'an and the history of Islam's growth have proven that Muslims must attempt to convert the world by using any tool; from the most gentle to the most ruthless. Islam does not leave people with the freedom to make their own religious decisions. The major strategic objective for faithful Muslims is to undermine the rights of every non-Islamic community in the world so that they cannot run their own societies according to their own cultural values. Everything outside of Islamic values is evil and must be wiped out from the surface of the earth. For this reason, wherever Muslims have invaded, they have eliminated the current systems of those places, burnt the libraries and books of that society and imposed their authoritarian system over it.

In some Islamic countries, Islam was not imported through direct invasions, but through laymen evangelists. However, regardless of the entry process, the spirit of jihad was in the essence of Islam and could not be separated from it. The spirit of jihad rose up in any community where there was a majority of Muslims, thus causing violence, force and pressures to be the overriding focus of every fanatical Muslim against native non-Muslims.

Islam is a severe religion in practice. This severity has made it extraordinarily estranged from both giving and using freedom in its real sense. In fact, the word "freedom" does not have an independent definition in the doctrine of Islam. It must always be defined in the shadow of Islam's fluctuating politics. That is why, in strongly religious oriented governments, freedom only means freedom to show allegiance to whatever the ruling government imposes on the residents. Rulers in Islamic countries, who do respect and protect personal freedom, are not relying totally on Islam. They prefer to leave behind the severity of Islam and adopt non-Islamic values for their society. We have seen and heard many times how fundamentalist Muslims in these countries hate these tolerant rulers, calling them Western agents and raising up riots against their tolerance toward other ideas. They also search for opportunities in order to assassinate them.

There were three reasons for Ayatollah Khomeini's protest in the 1970s against the king of Iran. First, he protested because of the king's failure to fully maintain Islamic values. Second, he accused the king of adapting Iran toward non-Islamic values, namely Western. Third, the king had accepted Israel as a country. The slogan, "down with the king," that the Ayatollah's followers were shouting in the streets was always accompanied with "down with America" and "down with Israel". This was mainly because the Ayatollah believed the king was friendly with America and America was helping Israel to grow stronger. Although, like all other governments of the world, the king had problems in his rule over Iran, this was not the major reason for the riots in Iran at that time by fundamentalist Muslims. Their motivation was only to turn the non-religious government into a religious one and in this way to "arrest and chain" freedom. But as became obvious after the 1979 Revolution in Iran, Khomeini's first call was apparently for Iran to be freed from the dictatorship of the king of Iran, who, he asserted, was a Western agent.

However, the calls he issued later were not in accord with his first call. His later calls showed that he wanted to establish a far stronger dictatorship and his rule became a threat toward other religions and ideas in Iran. One of his calls was to all of the Islamic scholars around the world, whom he wanted to undertake the destruction of all other religious centers other than Islam.[1] His successor, Ali Khamanei, also on another occasion called on many Islamic countries to prepare the ground for the creation of Islamic governments in all countries.[2] Similarly, what happened in Pakistan, Afghanistan, Indonesia, Sudan and in other Islamic countries against non-Muslims is in line with the objectives of Islam against freedom.

There are times in Islamic history when, to some extent, Muslims showed tolerance toward Christians and Jews. This tolerance was there only when the true followers of Islam did not have extensive religious power over the society and the society was run by more secular Muslims. However, the issue of Islamic fundamentalism was always a matter of fear for non-Muslims throughout the history of Islam. Fundamentalist Muslim invasions against the rights of non-Muslims are the result of calls and motivations that arise out of Islam. Nominal Muslims, on the other hand, are more tolerant and respectful toward the rights of others from different religious backgrounds, because they are less dependent on the calls of their religion.

The spirit of violence, force and pressure found in Islamic doctrine can be traced back to the very beginning of Muhammad's faith. You will remember from an earlier chapter that an angelic revelation was the starting point for Muhammad. The tradition says the following about this encounter. The angel Gabriel forced him to read the first verses of the Qur'an, while he was illiterate. The angel caught him forcefully and pressed him three times so hard, up to the point that his neck muscles twitched with terror. After the angel read the verses, Muhammad had no other choice but to repeat

---

1   M. Ayyubi (ed), *Khumeini Speaks Revelation*, (trans., N. M. Shaikh), Karachi: International Islamic Pub., 1981, P.25.

2   S. Bakhash, *The Reign of the Ayatollahs: Iran and the Islamic Revolution*, New York: Basic Books, 1984, P.235.

the angel's words.[1] Muhammad said this so that his followers would know that there is no choice when it comes to Islam; people have to follow Islam.

The spirit of Islam is the spirit of war and pressure any time it enters an individual's life or a society. It may be a silent or a riotous entry, but it always adapts and prepares Muslims gradually so that they ultimately express a spirit of fighting against non-Muslims.

Muhammad and his community believed in jihad for the establishment of God's kingdom on the earth. In contrast God's kingdom as taught by Jesus is not of this world:

> *Jesus answered, "My kingdom is not of this world. If My kingdom were of this world, My servants would fight, so that I should not be delivered to the Jews: but now My kingdom is not from here."* (John 18:36, also read Isaiah 9:6-7).

His disciple, Paul, said:

> *But beware lest somehow this liberty of yours become a stumbling block to those who are weak* (1 Corinthians 8:9).

The Bible says that the kingdom of heaven cannot be established by the sword and by the shedding of the blood of humankind:

> *Jesus said to him, "Put your sword back in its place ...* (Matthew 26:52).

> *For we do not wrestle against flesh and blood...* (Ephesians 6:12).

Therefore, the kingdom of God was established by God's love when Jesus took His stand to reconcile the world to God through love, against the devil's schemes of hatred, discord, fits of rage and the like:

> *He [God] has delivered us from the power of darkness ... For it pleased the Father in Him [Jesus} all the fullness should*

---

1 Ibn Hisham, *Sirat Rasul Allah,* P.209. & Also, read the narratives in Phil Parshall, *Inside the Community,* PP.18-21.

dwell, and by Him to reconcile all things to Himself, by Him, whether things on earth or things in heaven, having made peace through the blood of the His cross (Colossians 1:13, 20).

The works of the flesh are evident, which are: adultery, fornication, uncleanness, lewdness, idolatry, sorcery, hatred, contentions, jealousies, outbursts of wrath, selfish ambitions, dissensions, dissentions, heresies, envy, murders, drunkenness, revelries, and the like.... But the fruit of the Spirit is love, joy, peace, longsuffering, kindness, goodness, faithfulness, gentleness, self-control. Against such things there is no law. And those who are Christ's Jesus have crucified the flesh with its passions and desires (Galatians 5:19-24).

As is obvious, the kingdom of the Son Jesus Christ is represented by "love", whereas the kingdom of Muhammad is represented by the "sword". Muhammad said:

Paradise is under the shadow of the swords.[1]

The flag of Saudi Arabia, the heartland of Islam, carries the central message of the Qur'an, which is force. This grave and profound difference between Christian and Islamic doctrines has been causing Christians to suffer ever since the rise of Islam as a state religion. Muhammad announced himself as the absolute prophet for all and called all people, no matter whether they were monotheists or polytheists, to put their beliefs aside, even if good, and believe in Islam:

SAY to them: O men! Verily I am God's apostle to you all; ...the unlettered prophet... And follow him that ye may be guided aright (Q.7:158).

As a result of this, Christians and Jews also were asked to believe in Muhammad's new religion:

The true religion with God is Islam:... Abraham was neither Jew nor Christian; but he was sound in the faith, a Muslim;...

---

1 Muslim, Book 5, Hadith 1841. & Bukhari, Volume 2, Hadith 70.

Other religion than that of God desire they?… Whoso desireth any other religion than Islam, that religion shall never be accepted from him, and in the next world he shall be among the lost (Q.3:19, 67, 83, 85).

Those Christians and Jews who did not believe in Muhammad's message and did not join him or departed from him, were called enemies to Islam and consequently subject to death unless they signed a treaty and paid some tribute in order to live. In this way, those Christians and Jews who lived under the domination of Islam, became subject to different kinds of humiliations, threats and attacks from the rise of Islam until now (cf. Q.5:51; 9:29-30). Their beliefs and lives came to be seen as worthless and unlawful in the eyes of pious Muslims, merely because they chose not to submit to Islam. They were treated as strangers in their own lands and hometowns, and therefore, were killed or forced to pay tribute or leave.[1]

So Islam became an authoritarian religion and every one had to bow down before it. Those who did not embrace it, Muhammad stamped as infidels and did everything he could to convert them either by persuasion or by force.[2] As has happened with other authoritarian political systems throughout history, Islamic leaders searched for various excuses in order to legitimize the wiping out of those who thought differently and held other beliefs. Christians and Jews were not immune from the impact of these excuses. Muhammad held the contemporary Arabian Jews responsible for all the wrongdoings that the Jewish nation had committed from the exodus until the rise of Islam and he charged them with unbelief, mainly because they did not accept his prophecy. He said:

The last hour would not come unless the Muslims will fight against the Jews and the Muslims would kill them until the Jews would hide themselves behind a stone or a tree and a

---

1 For further information, read Colin Chapman, PP.283-289; quotations from Islamic traditions and contemporary writings.

2 K. Savage, P.122.

> *stone or a tree would say: Muslim, or the servant of Allah,*
> *there is a Jew behind me; come and kill him...* [1]

Similarly, Christians also suffered persecution under Islam but in a different way. Muhammad was aware of the tension between Jews and Christians. Some contemporary Christians accused Jews of rejecting Jesus and killing the prophets and Jews accused Christians of blasphemy for calling Jesus the Son of God. Muhammad, too, used the same accusations in his approach to Jews and Christians.

Another excuse to blame Christians was through using heretical Christian beliefs from church history. For example, there were always heretical beliefs, as early as the first century AD that spread to people from different nations and posed a threat to real Christianity. These heresies denied the deity, sonship and crucifixion of Jesus Christ. [2] These kinds of heretical ideas would have been familiar to Muhammad and some of his companions, because heretics were living everywhere Christians lived. An ancient Muslim researcher, who collected information from various religions and ideas for his book, wrote about the wide spread heretical Christian beliefs in Muhammad's time and explained why the Qur'an spoke negatively of two Christian sects, the Malkanites and Jacobites. [3] These heretical Christian ideas were used by Muslims to justify action by the law of the sword against Christianity. Christians were forced to acknowledge Muhammad's point of view, reducing the divine position of Jesus Christ to the level of his own manly politico-religious position. As a result, Christians were purged out of Arabia.

The success resulting from the war and violence against non-Islamic territories caused Islam's spirit of war and violence to become more impetuous and covetous, seeing the whole

---

1   Muslim, Book 41, Hadith 6985. & Bukhari, Volume 4, Book 52, Hadith 177.

2   ISB Encyclopedia, under the word "Heresy", PP.684-6.

3   A. M. A. Shahrestani, *Tozih-almelal*, PP.344,351 from book1.

world as its territory for invasion (the House of War or *Dar-al-Harb* in Arabic), in order to overcome all opponents. Ever since the rise of the Islamic state, the spirit of war and violence within Islam has been waiting to invade every person in the world, who for any reason dared to become critical toward Islam. Fundamental Muslims have always seen critics of their movement as an invasion of Islam's universal territory, and have called Muslims to target those who expressed the criticism, no matter what territorial rights and laws were in place to protect these individuals. Islam cannot stand up to any rational thinking and criticism because Allah desires so:

> *He* [Allah] *cannot be questioned for His acts, but people will be questioned (for theirs)* (Q.21. 23).

> [Their doom is] *because Allah sent down the Book* [Qur'an] *in truth but those who seek causes of dispute in the Book are in a schism far* [from the purpose] (Q.2:176).

> *Verily, you are those who have disputed about that of which you have knowledge. Why do you then dispute concerning that which you have no knowledge? It is Allah Who knows, and you know not* (Q.3:66).

> *…they* [unbelievers] *dispute about Allah. And he is mighty in strength and severe in punishment* (Q.13:13)

Teaching on Free Will

The same pressures that some pagan leaders in Mecca exerted on Muhammad, which he opposed, have unfortunately become the distinguishing characteristic of Muslim culture ever since Islam emerged as the state religion. Meccans accused Muhammad of disregarding the religion of his forefathers:

> *For when our distinct signs are recited to them, they say "This is merely a man who would fain pervert you from your father's worship." And they say, "This* [Koran] *is no other than a forged falsehood." And the unbelievers say to the truth when*

it is presented to them, *"Tis nothing but palpable sorcery"* (Q.34:43).

Later when Muhammad had succeeded, he treated others who drew back from Islam, deserting the faith, in a harsher manner than the Meccans had treated him:

> *O believers! make not friends of your fathers or your brethren if they love unbelief above faith: and whoso of you shall make them his friends, will be wrong doers* (Q.9:23).

> *O ye who believe! Verily, in your wives and your children ye have an enemy: wherefore beware of them. But if ye pass it over and pardon, and are lenient, then God is too Lenient, Merciful* (Q.64:14).

> *Give not way therefore to the Infidels, but by means of this Koran strive against them with a mighty strife* (Q.25:52).

> *O Prophet! make war on the infidels and hypocrites, and deal rigorously with them…* (Q.66:9).

Abubakr, Muhammad's successor (first caliphite) and father-in-law, who accompanied Muhammad when he invaded a Meccan caravan, became eager to shed the blood of his own son, Abdurahman, who did not accept Islam and had come with the Meccan warriors to protect the caravan from Muslims' invasion. He called his son a villain and impure and demanded back the portion of his wealth he had given his son. The son replied, "Why are you asking for wealth while the sword exists between you and me?" The incident turned into a bloody battle called *Badre*. At the beginning of the war, his son dared someone to fight him one on one. Abubakr, his father, accepted the challenge. When he realized it was his father that stepped forward, Abdurahman withdrew as a sign of cultural respect to his father whereas father proved through his action that he had already disregarded the culture of his own non-Islamic nation, the culture in which he grew.[1] When you become Muslim, you regard everything and everybody outside Islam as dead.

Ali, the forth caliphate and the holy leader of the Shiite sect, said, "Allah has commanded war against those who desert Islam."[2]

Islam teaches intolerance toward God-given free will. The above Qur'anic verses teach Muslims to be disrespectful toward their parents, siblings, wives and children if they choose not to be strong in following the footsteps of Muhammad. Even the Middle-Eastern cultural values stand against this disrespectful Islamic belief. Many Middle-Easterners love to keep the friendly aspects of their pre-Islamic cultures and have peaceful relationship with their family members and others. Their culture is older and nicer than the Islamic culture and for this reason some of them have been trying to protect it from the invasions of pious Muslims throughout the Islamic history. Therefore, Islam hasn't been able to fully ax the root of these friendly values because of peoples' perseverance in protecting their national values. However, Muhammad fought against these cultural values and left a legacy for his committed Muslims since the rise of Islam. Millions of moderate Muslims were killed by these committed Muslims in various parts of Islam's history because of their protective approaches towards their national culture and beliefs.

One Way Freedom

In Islam, you are free to become Muslim, follow its law or speak in favor of it, but not to criticize or leave it. Muhammad believed in his freedom to degrade his inherited pagan religion and leave it behind, but didn't believe in the freedom of Muslims to leave Islam or others to criticize it. He started his ministry by satirizing the leaders and their idols in Mecca, but never allowed others to question his deeds or religion after he

---

1   Ibn Hisham, *Sirat Rasul Allah,* P.575.

2   Salim Ibn-Ghaisse, *Asrar Aal Muhammad,* P.88.

got into power. His aggressive attitudes toward other beliefs became the sacred foundation for *Shari'a*, the way and law of Islam. To Islam the democratic laws are evil because they are based on peoples' decisions. Shari'a is based upon Allah and Muhammad; it is, therefore, the only legitimate source for ruling over the world. For this reason, the committed Muslims are obliged to fight the laws and values in every society through every possible way until Shari'a is established in that society. This is the reason that the committed Muslims in non-Islamic societies have been asking for the rule of Islam in their ghettos. They use (in reality abuse) the democratic philosophy in order to convince the democratic leaders and nations that like all other people group it is also their right to practice their religion. But in reality they do not believe in freedom and their goal is to replace the non-Islamic free values with the non-democratic Shari'a of Islam.

Muhammad's "one way" freedom philosophy penetrated Islamic institutions and individuals in all level and made them aggressive toward apostates and critics. It also has become a lurking and dangerous value in Islam's social and judiciary system, resulting in waves of assault against other cultures and beliefs. The limitation or banning of the activities of minor religions, the closure of their worship places and printing houses and the imprisonment and killing of their believers and leaders are all the result of this "one way" freedom in Islam.

In Islamic culture, no one has right to question anything of Islam.[1] Yet, as a Muslim in non-Islamic societies, you have right to criticize, disregard or demonize anything of their culture. Furthermore, your Islamic faith gives you right to even humiliate others. In contrast, when it comes to the Islamic arena, you are requested to show blind allegiance to everything from Islam. Islamic authorities prescribe limitless rights anytime, anywhere, anyway and over anybody, but when it comes to non-Muslims or even faithless Muslims the leaders

---

1   K. Cragg, P. 143.

never leave any space for them to express or exercise their rights. These kinds of values and beliefs have become strong parts of life in Islamic communities.

Muslim leaders have always believed that it is their right to continually criticize, discredit and invade Christian faith, books and beliefs, but Christians do not even have right to dispute about Islam, if they do they must be killed no matter the cost. For this reason, putting money for critics' heads is a popular practice in Islam.

Muslims are instructed to use everything they can for the destruction of freedom. Muhammad said:

> *Use your property, your persons any your tongues in striving against the polytheists.*[1]

Islamic evidences prove that the use of tongue (for lying or deception which is called holy or pious lying) against non-Muslims and their life values was the highest priority in Muhammad's approach to non-Muslims. With lies, he demonized them first and then legitimized to destroy them. He used every possible trick to destroy the freedom in Saudi Arabia.

Mecca was a free city open to every belief but Muhammad destroyed its freedom in a very subtle way. At the beginning of his migration to Medina, he did not have a strong army to invade Mecca and to change the lifestyle there. He, therefore, used his tongue as a cultural weapon. He legitimized that a faithful Muslim could even deny or denounce his faith for the sake of penetration so long as he was right in his heart with Allah. Arabs knew that they could use lies as weapons against their rival tribes, but it was strange for them to extend their lies to include their faith in god. You lied about everything if the condition necessitated, but it was disgusting to lie about your faith in the one you trusted. Muhammad legitimized this one too. Even some of his own companions got nervous and

---

1 Davud, Book 14, Hadith 2498.

unhappy for his openness to such a lie while he was signing a treaty with pagans, but he said to his companions that the false confession in the treaty was going to bring a victory for Muslims over pagans. The following hadith is about the treaty and his superficial denial of faith in Allah:

> *When Allah's Apostle concluded a peace treaty with the people of Hudaibiya, Ali bin Abu Talib wrote the document and he mentioned in it, "Muhammad, Allah's Apostle." The pagans said, "Don't write¹: "Muhammad, Allah's Apostle", for if you were an apostle we would not fight with you." Allah's Apostle asked Ali to rub it out, but Ali [Muhammad's son-in-law] said, "I will not be the person to rub it out." Allah's Apostle rubbed it out and made peace with them on the condition that the Prophet and his companions would enter Mecca and stay there for three days, and that they would enter with their weapons in cases.²*

In this hadith, we even read on how Muhammad's own son-in-law, Ali, was shocked because of Muhammad's lie about Allah and got angry at him. In the following hadith also, his father-in-law, Umar, was not happy but Muhammad convinces him that his lie was a victory for Islam:

> *[O]n the day of Hudaibiya, … Umar bin Al Khatab* [Muhammad's father-in-law] *came and said, "O Allah's Apostle! Aren't we in the right and our opponents in the wrong?" Allah's Apostle said, "Yes." Umar said, "Aren't our killed persons in Paradise and theirs in Hell?" He said, "Yes."* **Umar said, "Then why should we accept hard terms in matters concerning our religion?** *Shall we return before Allah judges between us and them?" Allah's Apostle said, "O*

---

1 Why were pagans not happy with Muhammad to write in the treaty "Allah's Apostle"? Because, Allah was the name of pagans' chief god, and they did not want Muhammad to use the name of their god for the god in his new religion, Islam.

2 Bukhari :: Volume 3 :: Book 49 :: Hadith 862 & Muslim :: Book 19 : Hadith 4401

Ibn Al-Khattab! I am the Apostle of Allah and Allah will never degrade me." Then Umar went to Abu Bakr [another father-in-law of Muhammad] *and told him the same as he had told the Prophet. On that Abu Bakr said* [to Umar]. *"He is the Apostle of Allah and Allah will never degrade him." Then Surat-al-Fath (i.e. Victory) was revealed and Allah's Apostle recited it to the end in front of Umar. On that Umar asked, "O Allah's Apostle! Was it* [i.e. the Hudaibiya Treat]) ***a victory?" Allah's Apostle said, "Yes".*[1] [Bold added.]

Immediately, after the treaty, the chapter 48 of the Qur'an, which is called the chapter (or surah) of "*Victory*" or *Al-Fath* in Arabic, was inspired in Muhammad by Allah as a confirmation that Muhammad's lie was a victory. The beginning verse of this chapter promises Muhammad that his sins (lies) will be forgiven.

Under the concept of *taqiyya* or *taghiyya* (holy lying), Muhammad and his followers are allowed even to deny their faith until they gain power in order to destroy their targeted society. He and his successor had peace treaties with one group at the expense of other groups. For example, because of the above treaty, pagans had no choice but to withdraw from defending the rights of Jews in Medina. Muhammad, therefore, had a chance to expel or kill Jewish males and seize all their females and possessions. He became rich as the result of this seizure and employed many soldiers, and soon after he disregarded the treaty with the pagans, invaded Mecca, killed many, destroyed all their idols and forced the whole region to accept Islam.

Committed Muslims cannot have peace with non-Muslims or even with faithless Muslims if they are in power. Only as minorities, they can have peace and that is until they gain power. Words like "democracy" and "freedom" are used by these committed Muslims, but these words do not carry any meaning for them unless they are used as cultural weapons

1 Bukhari, Volume 4, Book 53, Hadith 406.

for the destruction of their targeted communities. Even moderate Muslims know the deceptions behind the treaties of committed Muslims. They know how cleverly these pious followers of Muhammad deceive others. Sometimes, nominal Islamic governments speak or act in favor of these Muslims in order to appease dissidents and survive, though at the cost of minorities.

No Freedom of Speech and Religion

In an Islamic society, when religious values dominate all relationships, it even becomes dangerous to explore the paradoxical words of a religious leader.

When Ayatollah Khomeini returned to Iran in 1979, he gave his first speech in a famous cemetery in the capital city, Tehran. His aim in choosing this place was to assert that the Shah (king) had not brought progress to the country but had only brought progress to this cemetery by killing his oppositions. Using this as an object lesson he indirectly promised that he, contrary to the Shah's regime, would build the country and not the cemetery. This speech was powerful and had a positive effect on the people of Iran in supporting him both emotionally and politically. However a few months later, after gaining power for Islam, he himself became a "super slaughtering power" in Iran and made the cemetery ten times bigger than ever before. The country slipped backward but the cemetery went forward! This, of course, contradicted his first speech held in the cemetery, but no one had the right to criticize him for contradicting his promises. His agents started to remove his speeches from everywhere and it was a crime if someone had his cemetery speech or listened to it with a critical point of view.

While I was living in my home country, in one of my speeches I put forward the proposition that, for the benefit of the society, any wrong doing by anyone must not be ignored. Rather, the person doing these wrong acts who might even be the leader of the country, must be advised. I considered myself very lucky when I was able to escape the death penalty for making this speech. I only managed to do this by being accepted as a refugee in a non-Islamic country.

I can give you another example but this time from a minor Islamic community in a Christian country. An English man had an appointment with this ethnic community to discuss some issues. He was asked if he could arrange to bring along an interpreter, as this would help them to communicate together confidently. This person called me and asked for my help as an interpreter. I went with him and performed the task of interpreter. At the meeting there were two males from the community present, along with the English man and myself as interpreter. The discussion went on for a while and the two men decided that we needed a five-minute break for a cup of tea. During the tea time, they started talking to me in their own language. During our discussion they discovered that I was a Muslim who had converted to Christianity. Hearing this, they both paused for a few seconds and informed me that they didn't need me as an interpreter anymore. I reminded them that the meeting had not finished yet and my conversion was nothing to do with the interpretation I was called to do. They agreed that was the case, but they were not interested in working with an interpreter who could not keep his forefathers' religion, Islam. Whatever we (the English man and myself) tried to say to them in an effort to continue the second part of the discussion with them didn't work. They weren't interested because of my conversion to Christianity.

The English man asked them what was their motivation for breaching the right of equal opportunity and freedom in this democratic country by refusing to work with me as an interpreter? He asked them to give a reason why they as Muslims were happy to use the freedoms given to them by non-Muslims but were not happy to give any freedom to others. "According to the law of this country, we have been discriminated against by you. Do I have the right to call the police here or not?" he asked them. They did not answer his questions. The only thing they said to him in their broken English was, "*We need you come another time.*" They both turned their faces toward me and said to me in their own language, "*You are unclean; are you going to leave the building or do you want us to kick you out?*" They did not want to stay face to face with me anymore. Their pleasure was only to be found in my departure. In short, we both left.

Apparently, they both did not seem to be fundamentalist Muslims. However, as leaders of the community, they might have felt obligated to carry out the views of the community. This kind of fanatical mindset makes it difficult for some Muslims to accept the reality that people have freedom of choice in God's eyes.

Political, economic and social pressures were made legitimate in most Islamic societies in order to keep Muslims far from any opportunity for conversion. People are pushed to withdraw entirely from any Western model for society. That includes moving away from the freedom to uphold human rights with the loss of any respect for universal human rights. People are driven to become consistent in the practice of the Islamic way of life only.

This lack of freedom in Islamic culture has left it far behind in terms of meeting the natural needs of human life. There is always an uncertain and insecure feeling for every Muslim who becomes interested in sharing thoughts and opinions with non-Muslims, and living in peace with them.

The Love That Restores Peace

This lack of free will and choice is in direct contrast to the will of God revealed in the Bible. God took the initiative to restore peace and acceptance among people by giving Himself as an example through the love of His Son, Jesus Christ. In God's paradigm, love abounds regardless of allegiance:

"You have heard that it was said, 'You shall love your neighbor and hate your enemy.' But I say to you: Love your enemies, bless those who curse you, do good to those who hate you, and pray for those who spitefully use you and persecute you, "that you may be sons of your Father in heaven; for He makes His sun rise on the just and on the unjust. "For if you love those who love you, what reward have you? Do not even the tax collectors do the same? "And if you greet your brethren only, what do you do more than others? Don not even the tax collectors do so? "Therefore you shall be perfect, just as your Father in heaven is perfect (Matthew 5:43-48).

The courage for loving others finds its power in the Cross, where all the iniquities and inhuman activities of humanity were nailed so that the spirit of real freedom and love might be planted into the people's heart. The faith of the Son Jesus Christ respects the choice and free will of people. He believes that spiritual freedom requires the practice of free will through investigation and discovering the truth (John 8:32) that restores peace.

6

Who is the Savior of the Soul: God or Man?

What does the Qur'an Teach about Salvation?

Contradictions

Blameless God

Sinners, Oppressors and Losers

No One Is Able to Prevail

What Does the Qur'an Teach about Salvation?

Does the Qur'an believe in the lostness of humankind? Is salvation a major and serious issue in the Qur'an? Do Muslims console themselves with their own ability to work out salvation as the Qur'an teaches or do they cry to God to save them?

The Qur'anic evidence shows that companionship with Satan diverts mankind from God forever;

> *And whoso shall withdraw from the Warning of the God of Mercy, we will chain a Satan to him, and he will be his fast companion: For the Satan will turn men aside from the Way, who yet shall deem themselves rightly guided; Until when man shall come before us, he shall say, 'O Satan, would that between me and thee were the distance of the East and West.' And a wretched companion is a Satan* (Q.43:36-38).

The Qur'an also teaches that when Adam and Eve were deceived by Satan they were expelled out of Paradise (*Jannah*), were made enemies of one another and in this way they were lost:

> *So he* [Satan] *beguiled them* [Adam and Eve] *by deceit: and when they tasted of the tree, their nakedness appeared to them, and they began to sew together upon themselves the leaves of the garden. And their Lord called to them, 'Did I not say to you, "Verily, Satan is your declared enemy." They said, 'O our Lord! With ourselves have we dealt unjustly: if thou forgive us not and have pity on us, we shall surely be of those who perish.' He said, 'Get ye down, the one of you an enemy to the other;...O children of Adam! let not Satan bring you into trouble, as he drove forth your parents from the Garden* [Jannah] (Q.7:22-24,27).

Adam's and Eve's sin affected their children and descendants and made all sinners:

> *Verily Man is in loss* (Q.103:2).

Similarly Noah (Q.11:47; 71:27), Abraham (Q.14:41), Moses (Q.7:151; 26:82; 28:16) and Muhammad (Q.47:19; 48:2) all call themselves sinners in the Qur'an and show concern for the result of their own sins and ask God to forgive them. Only Jesus is perfect and holy according to the Qur'an (Q.19:18-19); He is the Word and Spirit of God (Q.4.171b; 19:17); He is the proof of resurrection (Q.43:61); He is in heaven (Q.4:158) and will come again and judge the world at the end (c.f. Q.3:55; 4:158).[1]

The Qur'an states that no one except God will be able to help the sinner:

> *Not according to your wishes, or the wishes of the people of the Book, shall these things be. He who does evil shall be recompensed for it. Patron or helper, beside of God, shall he find none* (Q.4:123)

How does God help the sinner in order to be saved? Is it through the direct revelation of God or through the human agent?

There are verses in the Qur'an and in the Bible which bring forth the meaning that the descendants of Adam and Eve cannot be trusted because of their sinful nature:

> *Verily, we proposed to the Heavens, and to the Earth, and to the Mountains to receive the Faith, but they refused the burden, and they feared to receive it. Man undertook to bear it, but has proved unjust, senseless* (Q.33:72)!

> *There is none righteous, no, not one* (Romans 3:10).

> *Cursed is the man who trusts in man and makes flesh his strength, whose heart departs from the LORD* (Jeremiah 17:5).

This is because of the spiritual loss that resulted from their rebellious nature against God. Although God calls and

---

1 Also read; A. M. A. Shahrestani, *Tozih-almelal*, P.340.

chooses some of these earthly and sinful people and uses them to announce His message and plan of salvation, He never abandons the plan of salvation into their hands. He rather undertakes it through His own Word and Spirit (Jesus) who is from heaven. God is pleased when people trust in the One who comes from heaven for salvation rather than in anyone who is from the earth.

Why has God chosen this way? Because the One who is from heaven is God's own Spirit, who is above all, and able to save people. He differs completely in essence from anyone who is from the earth. The one from the earth has inherited the corrupt qualities of Adam and Eve and therefore is lost and in need of a Savior. The One who has come from heaven is "the Word and the Spirit" of God, and therefore, can reveal the will, truth and glory of God into a person's life (see John 1:1-3, 14). That is why Jesus says, *"He who has seen me has seen the Father"* (John 14:9).

The possibility for people to be saved when they rely on the One who is from heaven is one hundred per cent. Reliance on anyone who is from the earth makes salvation impossible. From the Bible and the Qur'an we understand that the essence of Jesus is from heaven and is purely good, but Moses or Muhammad, both descendants of Adam and Eve, are sinful. This is God's logical reason for Jesus being called sinless and trustworthy, while all other prophets are called sinners and incomparable with Jesus. It was these characteristics of Jesus Christ that sealed the prophetic line with His essence and provided such an opportunity that people could come face to face with God rather than only hearing about Him. God provided people with a heavenly opportunity so they could personally put their hands in His hands. How can a man who is the descendant of Adam and Eve, and thereby lost in the sinful world, be trusted for this position of reconciliation? "They cannot be trusted" is the message of the Bible. Only Jesus can be trusted:

> *This* [Jesus] *is the stone which was rejected by you builders, which has become the chief cornerstone. Nor is there salvation in any other, for there is no other name under heaven given among men by which we must be saved* (Acts 4:11-12).

Also, the Bible, unlike the Qur'an, introduces God as the One who does not want to leave the problem of sin for the life after. God is zealous to wipe out the problems of sin now. Furthermore, He does not want people to suffer the fault of their parents, Adam and Eve, on earth and into eternity. The problem, which arose in this world, must be reckoned with and resolved in this world. It is here on earth that humankind must be brought back to their original state and enjoy life with God. For this reason, Jesus Christ took responsibility on the Cross for the sins of the world in order to reconcile God and humankind.

We need to be transferred from the dominion of darkness into God's kingdom so we can have an intimate relationship with God and live in harmony with His personality and will. This transformation simply means: to be with God and in God; to live and act in God. How can a rebellious and sinful man, who is lost and dead in the eyes of God and deserves not to be with Him, be transformed into God's kingdom and enabled to live for God? Who will be the best person to undertake this ministry of transformation; the one who is from earth (sinful person), or the One who is from heaven (the Spirit or the Word of God)? Anyone who loves justice and holiness will certainly vote for the Spirit who is sinless, and who came down from heaven and revealed Himself in Jesus Christ. Therefore, all humankind, including Muslims, need to listen to the cry of their conscience for salvation and allow the Spirit of Christ, who is from heaven, to remove the barriers in front of them and reconcile them with God and make them victorious over Satan. In Jesus not only we are protected from Satan but we have conquered him too (Colossians 2:13-15; Romans 8:37).

Contradictions

As it was stated earlier, the Qur'an does not always hold one particular view about an issue. The Qur'an's ideas about salvation are subject to this instability. Therefore, it is impossible to derive a perfect plan for salvation from the verses of the Qur'an.

The Qur'an encourages its followers to be good and do right so that they might enter heaven after death. Yet it states that everybody, both righteous and unrighteous, will be first led to hell by Allah!:

> *And observe prayer at early morning, at the close of the day, and at the approach of night; for the good deeds drive away the evil deeds...* (Q.11:114).

> *Doth not man bear in mind that we made him at first, when he was nought? And I swear by the Lord, we will surely gather together them and Satans: then will we set them on their knees round Hell: Then will we take forth from each band those of them who have been stoutest in rebellion against the God of Mercy: Then shall we know right well to whom its burning is most due: No one is there of you who shall not go down unto it - This is settled decree with thy Lord - Then will we deliver those who had the fear of God, and the wicked will we leave in it on their knees* (Q.19:67-72).

This is contrary to the Gospel of Jesus Christ. God has created a great chasm between hell and heaven as a matter of protection for the righteous (Luke 16:26). The Bible teaches that the righteous must be kept safe from the effect of hell forever, from the time of faith placed in the Son, Jesus Christ. Any person who comes to Christ has eternal life; hell and its sting is swallowed up in victory forever (1 Corinthians 15:53-57). This is the major work of the Son Jesus Christ. Every prophet before Jesus expected Him to enter the world and to undertake this saving act. Both New and Old Testaments in the Bible prove how people become victorious over eternal death by believing in Jesus, the Son of God (Isaiah 25:8; 53; Revelation 20:14-15).

However, despite the above contradictions in the Qur'an, Islam teaches that fallen man is capable of saving himself through good deeds. It is not for God to come to man and save him; man is called to save himself and go to God. *This is one of the major differences between Islam and Christianity.* Islam asks personal man (though in chains) to go to impersonal god, but in the Bible personal God comes to personal man in order to unchain him. Though in the Qur'an Allah has been introduced as compassionate, his compassion does not mean, as in Christianity, that he stretches his hands to save the lost. He is called compassionate only because he shows man how to rely on his own good deeds for salvation. What good things does Allah expect from a chained man? If man is not freed from the kingdom of sin, he will not be able to do good. Even if we imagine that man can save himself, the salvation of God is more trustworthy than the salvation of man, as it is in the Bible. In Islam man is the savior, but in Christianity God is the Savior.

The disunity among the verses of the Qur'an's about salvation, and other Islamic texts have made Islam the most uncertain religion in the world. Aisha, Muhammad's youngest wife, said:

> *Whoever tells you that the Prophet knows what is going to happen tomorrow, is a liar. She then recited: 'No soul can know what it will earn tomorrow.* [Q.31:34][1]

Muhammad said:

> *"The good deeds of any person will not make him enter Paradise." The Prophet's companions said, "Not even you, O Allah's Apostle?" He said, "Not even myself, unless Allah bestows His favor and mercy* [rahma]*_on me.*"[2]

---

1 Bukhari, Volume 6, Book 60, Hadith 378.
2 Bukhari, Volume 7, Book 70, Hadith 577. & Q.46:9.

Muslim theologians wonder about how to deal with the conflicting views presented within Islamic manuscripts. They wonder about which ideas to promote; the importance of man's good deeds flowing from the exercise of his free will, or the will of Allah who ignores the work of people but assigns paradise for some and hell for others? Narrated Ali:

> *We were in the company of the Prophet and he said, "There is none among you but has his place written for him, either in Paradise or in the Hell-Fire." We said, "O Allah's Apostle! Shall we depend* [on this fact and give up work]*?" He replied, "No! Carry on doing good deeds, for everybody will find easy* [to do] *such deeds as will lead him to his destined place." Then the Prophet recited: "As for him who gives* [in charity] *and keeps his duty to Allah, and believes in the Best reward. We will make smooth for him the path of ease...the path for evil."*[1]

> *"We were accompanying a funeral procession in Baqi-I-Gharqad. The Prophet came to us and sat and we sat around him. He had a small stick in his hand then he bent his head and started scraping the ground with it. He then said, "There is none among you, and not a created soul, but has place either in Paradise or in Hell assigned for him and it is also determined for him whether he will be among the blessed or wretched." A man said, "O Allah's Apostle! Should we not depend on what has been written for us and leave the deeds as whoever amongst us is blessed will do the deeds of a blessed person and whoever amongst us will be wretched, will do the deeds of a wretched person?" The Prophet said, "The good deeds are made easy for the blessed, and bad deeds are made easy for the wretched." Then he recited the Verses:-- "As for him who gives* [in charity] *and is Allah-fearing And believes in the Best reward from Allah."*[2]

---

1 Bukhari, Volume 6, Book 60, Hadith 472. & Q.92:5-10.
2 Bukhari, Volume 2, Book 23, Hadith 444.

Allah leaves his most beloved man, Muhammad, even in uncertainty. This is not the message of Jesus Christ. He gives certainty:

> *Most assuredly, I say to you, , he who hears My word and believes in Him who sent Me has everlasting life, and shall not come into judgment, but has passed from death into life* (John 5:24).

If man is destined to be active and responsible for his own salvation, why then should he be left uncertain about his salvation, especially when he has tried his best to be victorious prior to his death? The following verses of the Qur'an illustrate the uncertainty of Muhammad's own spiritual future:

> *SAY: I* [Muhammad] *have no control over what may be helpful or hurtful to me, but as God wills. Had I the knowledge of his secrets, I should revel in the good, and evil should not touch me. But I am only a warner, and an announcer of good tidings to those who believe* (Q.7:188).

> *SAY: I* [Muhammad] *am no apostle of new doctrines: neither know I what will be done with me or you. Only what is revealed to me do I follow, and I am only charged to warn openly* (Q.46:9).

Why does Allah contradict himself and withdraw from the promises he has made to his righteous followers? Why would Muhammad, who is called the seal of the prophets, the most righteous of all and the best example for all, not be able to believe in salvation for himself? Why does he deliver such a worrisome message to his followers? Who is the cause of this unbelief and uncertainty? Is there any benefit in uncertainty, for which Allah has ordained his people? Why would the Qur'an authorize Muhammad to call people to follow in his footsteps, when he is uncertain about his own future? How could a person guide people to future while he himself is uncertain about his future? Why would the Qur'an give authority to Muhammad to judge against anyone who has failed to obey him or give allegiance to him who himself does not have assurance of salvation?

> *SAY: If ye* [people] *love God, then follow me* [Muhammad]*: God will love you, and forgive your sins, for God is forgiving, Merciful. SAY: Obey God and the Apostle; but if you turn away, then verily, God loveth not the unbelievers* (Q.3:31).

> *As for those who were infidels and turned others aside from the way of God, to them we will add punishment on punishment for their corrupt doings. And one day we will summon up in every people a witness against them from among themselves; and we will bring thee up as witness against these Meccans: for to thee have we sent down the Book which cleareth up everything, a guidance, and mercy, and glad tidings to those who resign themselves to God* [to Muslims] (Q.16:88-89).

What a contradiction? How does the spirit of evangelism in these verses match with the uncertainty of the verses Q.7:188; 46:9? How could the uncertainty in Islam lead to the "glad tidings" expressed in Q.16:89?

Why does the Qur'an call Muslims the best of all humankind, having the ability and power to guide (order) all other people unto righteousness, keeping them away from unbelief, when Muslims are put in an uncertain and passive situation by the Qur'an itself?:

> *Ye* [Muslims] *are the best folk that had been raised up unto mankind* (Q.3:110).

Versus

> *...Nor does anyone know what it is that he will earn tomorrow* (Q.31:34).

If there were spiritual excellence, perfection and paradise in Islam could they go with confusion and uncertainty? Then how are Muslims able to open a door to help other people while Allah has not yet opened the door to his own people on earth?

Assurance of salvation is the central message of the Bible for the life on earth. A real God does not leave people in uncertainty. Although Satan was able to bring sin into man's life and separate him from eternal life, God is mightier because He can drive out Satan from man's life and take him back to eternal life. We are offered this assurance from Christ and can experience the reality of this exchanged life on earth. Allah does not have it, therefore, he can neither offer it, nor can Muslims receive it from him.

The Bible, contrary to the Qur'an, teaches that fallen man must first rise from the fallen state. Rebellious man has broken relationship with God and consequently established relationship with Satan. Relationship with God and Satan simultaneously is impossible; relationship with one means separation from the other. Satan, unlike God, does not believe in freedom. For this reason, he blinds them to the truth. His plan is to chain his companions in his kingdom forever. The only source that can break this chain is God. Sin results in slavery to Satan and renders a person weaker than Satan. Self-rescue from the hand of Satan is impossible. But God transfers anyone who asks Him for Salvation into His kingdom (see Romans 6:20-23).

In Christianity God saves people and brings them back to himself during the life on earth. Salvation is man's main need and Jesus Christ is the One to save. He is the Lord of Salvation and His Gospel is the power for salvation of everyone who believes in Him (see Acts 4:12, Romans 1:16). The Gospel of Christ says, *"for all have sinned and fall short of the glory of God, being justified freely by His grace through the redemption that is in Christ Jesus"* (Romans 3:23-24). This just, holy and kind God reaches out to rescue humanity, whom He has created for Himself, giving them the certainty of eternal life in this world for the world to come.

God created Adam and Eve good and for Himself. Satan caused them to sin and to fall far from God. God revealed in His triunity (the Trinity)as the *Father* to have His children back to relationship with Him; as the *Son* to remove the barriers; as the *Holy Spirit* to run the life journey with His beloved ones to the end. The **love** of God took the initiative to bring people back (John 3:16). His **justice** entered the world to rescue them from the dominion of darkness and to bring them back home to be with their Creator and God (Colossians 1:13; Romans 5:1). His **holiness** (the Holy Spirit) also seals and guarantees their heavenly inheritance (Ephesians 1:14; 4:30).

Allah Who Misleads

The following verses of the Qur'an clearly prove that some of Allah's deeds are not different but complementary to Satan's work with humankind. Allah disables men and women in order to promote the kingdom of darkness in the same way as Satan. These verses prove that humankind is caught up in the unstable will of Allah that diminishes the will of humans below what had been ordained for them in the beginning. He sometimes strengthens Satan, hands over people to him, or calls them back to himself:

> *SAY: Nothing can befall us but what Allah hath destined for us* (Q.9:51).

> *God hath set a seal upon their[1] hearts: they have no knowledge* (Q.9:93).

> *Why are ye two parties on the subject of the hypocrites, when Allah has cast them off for their doings? Desire ye to guide those whom God hath led astray? But for him whom Allah leadeth astray, thou shalt by no means find a pathway* (Q.4:88 and cf. 35:8; 74:31).

> *Many, moreover, of the jinn and men have we created for Hell. Heart have they with which they understand not, and eyes have they with which they see not, and ears have they with*

---

1 Those who do not believe, stay behind, and do not fight for the cause of Islam.

which they hearken not. They are like the brutes: Yea, they go more astray: these are heedless (Q.7:179).

Had thy Lord pleased he would have made mankind of one religion (community): *but those only to whom thy Lord has granted his mercy will cease to differ. And unto this hath He created them; for the word of thy Lord shall be fulfilled, "I will wholly fill hell with jinn and men"* (Q.11:118-119).

God misleads whom He will, and whom He will he guides: and He is the mighty, the Wise (Q.14:4).

Had we [God] pleased we had certainly given to every soul its guidance. But true shall be the word which hath gone forth from me - I will surely fill hell with jinn and men together (Q.32:13).

Before them [infidels] *have we [Allah] set a barrier and behind them a barrier, and we have shrouded them in a veil, so that they shall not see. Alike is it to them if thou warn them or warn them not: they will not believe* (Q.36:9-10).

Had God pleased, He could have made you one people: but He causes whom He will to err, and whom He will He guides: and ye (all) *shall assuredly be called to account for your doings* (Q.16: 93).

And whoso shall withdraw from the Warning of the God of Mercy, we will chain a Satan to him, and he will be his fast companion: For the Satan will turn men aside from the Way, who yet shall deem themselves rightly guided; Until when man shall come before us, he shall say, "O Satan, would that between me and thee were the distance of the East and West." And a wretched companion is a Satan (Q.43:36-38).

So he [Satan] beguiled them [Adam and Eve] by deceit: and when they tasted of the tree, their nakedness appeared to them, and they began to sew together upon themselves the leaves of the garden. And their Lord called to them, "Did I not say to you, 'Verily, Satan is your declared enemy.'" *They said,*

'O our Lord! With ourselves have we dealt unjustly: if thou forgive us not and have pity on us, we shall surely be of those who perish.'" He said, "Get ye down, the one of you an enemy to the other;...O children of Adam! let not Satan bring you into trouble, as he drove forth your parents from the Garden" [Jannah] (Q.7:22-24,27).

What does right and wrong mean in Islam? Are right and wrong two independent values through which the two different kingdoms of God and Satan can be distinguished from each other? Or, are they unified in one kingdom working side by side? Does Allah lead astray and guides in truth with the same essence? What does the true and straight path mean in the theology of the Qur'an? Is it the mixture of bad and good?

Guide Thou us on the straight path (Q.1:6)

Unfortunately, the Qur'an presents Satan more honest than Allah. Satan mission is only to lead people to evil, but Allah's goal is to lead them both to good and evil. Like pagan gods, Allah has two opposite hearts; on one hand he paves the ground for people to get lost but on the other hand calls them to come back. On one hand, he asks them to do good, but on the other hand he disregards their good deeds or leaves them in uncertainty. If Allah, at the end, can disregard people's good deeds, which he himself has recommended them to do, then what benefits people will reap from doing good deeds? If Allah bases salvation upon man's good deeds then what are this contradiction in the Qur'an for? Why should people be held accountable for the bad deeds which were inspired in them by Allah? What is the benefit of religion, its rituals, its requirements, etc. if none can help Muslim to survive at the end? Why would Muslims be interested in waging jihad (war) against those whom Allah has chosen to stay unbelievers but their own faults? Why does Allah take delight in shedding the blood of those whose unbelief is from Allah himself? Where does justice fit in the call and cause of Allah? We know that even the most elegant words in the Qur'an have left these questions unanswered. Islam intends to have the world, but with a confused theology.

Not only says the Quran that Allah is the creator of sin and corruption but so do the Hadiths, the words of Muhammad:

> *Allah, the Blessed, the Exalted, created Adam. Then He stroked his back with His right hand, and progeny issued from it. He said, "I created these for the Garden and they will act with the behaviour of the people of the Garden." Then He stroked his back again and brought forth progeny from him. He said, "I created these for the Fire and they will act with the behaviour of the people of the Fire." A man said, "Messenger of Allah! Then of what value are deeds'" The Messenger of Allah, may Allah bless him and grant him peace, answered, "'When Allah creates a slave for the Garden, he makes him use the behaviour of the people of the Garden, so that he dies on one of the actions of the people of the Garden and by it He brings him into the Garden. When He creates a slave for the Fire, He makes him use the behaviour of the people of the Fire, so that he dies on one of the actions of the people of the Fire, and by it, He brings him into the Fire."*[1]

The following Hadith is also saying that it is Allah who created some for heaven and some others for hell:

> *There was an argument between Adam and Moses in the presence of their Lord. Adam came the better of Moses. Moses said: "Are you that Adam whom Allah created with His Hand and breathed into him His sprit, and commanded angels to fall in prostration before him and He made you live in Paradise with comfort and ease. Then you caused the people to get down to the earth because of your lapse." Adam said: "Are you that Moses whom Allah selected for His Messengership and for His conversation with him and conferred upon you the tablets, in which everything was clearly explained and granted you the audience in order to have confidential talk with you. What is*

---

1 Malik , Book 46, Hadith 46.1.2 .

your opinion, how long Torah would have been written before I was created?" Moses said: "Forty years before." Adam said: "Did you not see these words: Adam committed an error and he was enticed to [do so]." He [Moses] said: "Yes." Whereupon, he [Adam] said: "Do you then blame me for an act which Allah had ordained for me forty years before He created me?" Allah's Messenger [may peace be upon him] said: "This is how Adam came the better of Moses."[1]

Thought this Hadith is not translated properly, however, it is trying to say that Allah ordained sin for Adam forty years before he created Adam. In other words, sin in Islam comes from Allah, it is pre-historical and eternal. This is what pagans believe and teach.

Sin Is Eternal in Islam

Islam teaches that sin was ordained by Allah for humanity before creation, was put into practice in the life of people by Allah in creation and therefore is with humanity by Allah until they die.

Islam has two major doctrinal problems here. Firstly, it attributes the ordination and creation of sin to God. God is holy in essence and therefore perfectly away from sin. It is impossible for Him to create or ordain sin. This shows that the god in Islam cannot be real, but only a god made in the image of Muhammad.

Secondly, if sin is ordained before creation, it means that sin is eternal and does not have a beginning. Muslims also believe that Allah is eternal and does not have a beginning. Philosophically and doctrinally we know that there cannot be two eternal or infinite (∞) things without a beginning, but only God. The real meaning of Islamic belief is that Allah, the infinite one (∞) is the same as the infinite (∞) sin. In other words, Allah and sin

---

1 Muslim, Book 33, Hadith 6411.

are the same. We know that the true God is not sin. Therefore, Allah is not the true God.

In their conversations with Christians, Muslims do not believe that there is an original sin starting from Adam and penetrating into the life of their descendants, humanity. They discuss this in order to convince Christians that sin cannot come from Adam to his descendants, but sin is stealing, debauchery, adultery, etc. that each person does and is responsible to purify himself and stay away from sin. Unfortunately, they do not understand that in Islam no one can stay away from a sin which is eternal, beyond the original sin (of Adam) and created by Allah's hands. Also, it was not Adam's fault when he sinned, because Allah had ordained him with sin before he was created. Allah also ordained all with sin (Q.91:7-8).

Islamic theologians (*Ibn-Hazm* for example) ponder the elegant and beautiful words such as holiness, justice, righteousness, love, forgiveness, etc., mentioned in the Qur'an. They say that these words cannot be used theologically and they are unable to understand their real meaning and cannot explain why they are in the Qur'an. They have to use these words in their daily talks, not because they are relevant to and useful in their lives, but because these words are in the Qur'an and cannot be taken out.[1] They say this because they are confused on how the creator of these elegant words, Allah, created sin too.

Allah is the giver of both good and evil. He himself corrupted Satan from the beginning so that he could corrupt people:

> *He* [Satan] *said, "Now, for that thou* [Allah] *hast caused me to err, surely in thy straight path will I lay wait for them* [humankind]*: Then will I surely come upon them from before, and from their left, and thou shalt not find the greater part of them to be thankful." He said, "Go forth from it, a scorned, a banished one! Whoever of them shall follow thee, I will surely fill hell with you, one and all"* (Q.7:16-18).

---

1 G. Nehls, *Christians Ask Muslims*, P. 28.

Also, Allah inspired (breathed) the sin into man's soul to make him vulnerable to fall into the dominion of Satan:

> *By a Soul and Him who balanced it, And* [Allah] *breathed into it its wickedness[1] and its piety, Blessed now is he who hath kept it pure* (Q.91:7-9).

Muhammad said:

> *Had you not committed sins, Allah would have brought into existence a creation that would have committed sin* [and Allah] *would have forgiven them.[2]*

> *By Him in whose Hand is my life, if you were not to commit sin, Allah would sweep you out of existence and He would replace* [you by] *those people who would commit sin and seek forgiveness from Allah, and He would have pardoned them.[3]*

> *No child is born but that Satan touches it when it is born whereupon it starts crying loudly because of being touched by Satan, except Mary and her Son[4].*

Allah first causes the fall of humanity and then calls them to repent and ask for forgiveness. Why should people repent to Allah for the problem he himself is the cause? Shouldn't Allah apologize to people since he has brought sin into their lives? Allah leads people into the darkness and then asks them to follow the truth. This seems very shocking! Is there any trace of truth in the kingdom of darkness to motivate people to follow the truth?

---

1 The word in Arabic is "fojooraha" which means debauchery.

2 Sahih Al-Musim *Hadith* No.1277

3 Sahih Al-Musim Hadith No.1278

4 Dr. Muhammad Muhsin Khan, *Sahih Bukhari Vol.6, Hadith 71,* Published by Islamic University, Al Medina Al Munauwara, P.54, ND.

Blameless God

The God of the Bible is holy and just. He therefore cannot be the cause of sin and confusion. Adam and Eve were created holy and sinless by God. It was not God who inspired sin in them. They listened to Satan and sinned against the holy God. God in His mercy attracted their attention and paved the ground for them to receive His plan for reconciliation and unity.

God of the Holy Bible calls to men and women, and says, "*Come now, let us reason together*" (Isaiah 1:18). (Let us see who is right, who is sinner who is the cause of all problems.) God does not want people to stay unaware or follow Him blindly (see John 8:32). He has created man and woman in His likeness with free will, and enabled them to test and choose freely. They have God-given capacity to comprehend the goodness and distinguish it from evil (see Romans 8:20).

Muslims need to search and see that the God of the Bible is blameless, and He never leads His creatures to hell. He is the source and giver of all good. They have to call upon the true God who is purely good and has no evil desires. A pure and holy God cannot create evil. If a Muslim truly desires and is prepared to seek for the true God, he will absolutely find Jesus Christ as his Lord, because the Gospel of Jesus does not teach about dualist god (the creator of bad and good), instead it teaches:

> *The wisdom that is from above is first pure, then peaceable, gentle, willing to yield, full of mercy and good fruit, without partiality and without hypocrisy* (James 3:17).

God of the Bible is HOLY and PURE and whatever comes from Him is also pure. Our salvation will be guaranteed if we rely on the holy and pure God. There is a grave distinction between the God who is the giver of all good, and the god who is the giver of both good and evil. Anyone, who comes to discover this difference between Christianity and Islam, would eagerly follow the footsteps of Jesus Christ, the Son. Those who desire to relate themselves to the Holy God, will find that they need to relate themselves first to Jesus Christ. He is the Way to God (John 14:6). The inherent goodness in Him has made Him the Master and the Lord of eternal life. He therefore is worthy of leading people to eternal life. He is in heaven and is able to draw people to heaven.

Sinners, Oppressors and Losers

The effect of sin is beyond all imagination. No one can be freed from sin by his/her own power. Man gives up eventually if he tries to rely on his own power. That is why the pressure of sin on Muhammad's life cause him to give up his trust in his good deeds and live as a spiritually wondering man:

> *...neither know I what will be done with me or you...* (Q.46:9)

Satan is openly an enemy of humankind. His job is to lead humankind to a life without God and salvation. The Qur'an says that all people, including prophets, are sinners, oppressors, and losers:

> *Verily, man's lot is cast amid destruction* (Q.103:2).

> *Man...has proved unjust, senseless* (Q.33:72).

Muslims cry to Allah five times a day and repeat ten times the following:

> *Guide Thou us on the straight path, the path of those to whom you hast been gracious; with whom thou are not angry, and who go not astray¹* (Q.1:6-7).

Muslims ask Allah to have mercy on them and rescue them from the eternal death. Some of them pray seventy years, crying to Allah to put them in the right path, but Allah leaves them with uncertainty for the life after. If Allah was a loving God, he would have a mother's or father's heart and would hurry to help

---

1   "Zaallin" in Arabic, which equals misled, lost, wandered and those who went astray.

and save. If a child cries to mother or father for help, parents do not leave the need of their child for the life after; they instead rush and meet the need of their child immediately. A true God does the same.

This is the grave difference between the Qur'an and the Bible; the Bible saves but the Qur'an leaves for the life after, though with uncertainty.

No One Is Able to Prevail

Muslims do not realize that no one is able to prevail through one's own strength. They are all unconsciously obeying a falsehood that is leading them to more sufferings. Their attempts to reach God do not have a place in God's plan of salvation. Salvation is the exodus from the dominion of Satan to the kingdom of God. Although the human heart desires for such a release, the corrupt soul acts as an obstacle in the way to freedom. There is a conflict in the soul of humankind between accepting grace and continuing in corruption, between the law of God in which they delight and to which they want to conform, and the law of sin, which is also appealing. The law of sin captivates and compels us to do that which we do not want to do.[1] Corrupt tendencies in the heart of all humankind preclude us from appearing without any sin in the presence of God. The way to salvation is, therefore, unattainable by man.

It is obvious that Muslims, like many other nations of the world, love God and try hard to reach Him so that their distance from God might be abolished. Although the mainstream culture in Islamic societies says "God is with us", the writings of the Qur'an prove to us that God and Muslims are not able to be with each other. If they were with God, they would be in the kingdom of God (paradise) and would not have any need for the daily rituals, prayers and practices in order to store up righteousness for the Day of Judgment. Therefore, there is a distance between Muslims and God which has caused them to

---

1   Iskandar Jadeed, P.4. & cf. Rom. 7:18-23.

cry and try their best so that they may receive salvation after life. Sadly, they do not know that mankind cannot prevail by their own power. They also do not know that it breaks God's heart while He is ready to save them but they rely on their own power for this. That is why God says in the Bible:

> *Cursed is the man who trusts in man, and makes flesh his strength, whose heart departs from the LORD. For he shall be like as shrub in the desert, and shall not see when good comes, but shall inhabit the parched places in the wilderness, in a salt land which not inhabited. Blessed is the man who trusts in the LORD, and whose hope is the LORD. For he shall be like a tree planted by the waters, which spreads out its roots by the river, and will not fear when heat comes; but its leaf will be green, and will not be anxious in the year of drought, nor will cease from yielding fruit* (Jeremiah 17:5-8).

Sin has corrupted everyone and has chained all in the prison of darkness. There is no hope of light and salvation in the darkness. Also, the prince of darkness , Satan, does not believe in salvation and freedom, but God does. God is mighty and is able to free us from Satan. If we accept His **perfect plan in Jesus Christ,** we will be saved.

7

How can Muslims Follow Jesus, the Son of God?

*Through the Active Word and
Love of the Son*

Through the Messengers of the Son

Evangelism Is Possible among Muslims

Through the Active Word and Love of the Son

The Apostle Paul said, *"It* [the Gospel] *is the power of God to salvation for everyone who believes"* (Romans 1:16). The core meaning of the Gospel is described in 1 Corinthians 15:3-4 by Paul: *". . . that Christ died for our sins according to the Scriptures, and that He was buried, and that He rose again the third day according to the Scriptures."* There are many ramifications of the Gospel that empowered Paul's life and empower the lives of Christ's followers today. Paul said that the proclamation of the word of Christ delivered him from the lion's mouth (2 Timothy 4:17). He wrote this because he experienced the power of the Gospel in every event of his ministry from the time he came to faith in Christ to the end. There was not a single experience in his ministry that disillusioned him about being a spokesman for Christ. The active word, love and humility of Christ in him humbled his enemies at the feet of Christ, just as had happened to him. We read in the Gospel that even a jailer washed the wounds that the chains had left on Paul's body (see Acts 16:33).

Those who have tasted the pain of being in a bitter and harsh jail know the severity of a harsh jailer. In jails like these such as jails I have experienced in the Islamic Republic of Iran, a jailer is appointed to this position in order to give prisoners as much emotional and physical pain and persecution as possible. He has to be a person who enjoys the pain of his prisoners. He must be able to dig into the already existing wounds on the prisoner's body in order to increase the pain to an even higher level. He tortures, rapes, kills and does everything that might help to change the prisoner's mindset. When a jailer such as this humbles himself and comes to follow the faith of his humiliated prisoner, there must be a loving and changing power in the message of that prisoner. This effect on jailers is what Christian prisoners have been seeing in the prisons of various countries ever since the rise of Christianity.

There is indeed power in the loving message of Jesus Christ that even amazes the most brutal people and causes them to change their mindset. The history of Christianity has recorded amazing testimonies of how the enemies of Christ turned and became His friends and followers. Paul's life is evidence of this. He had a strong hatred toward Christians. This led him to be a violent persecutor of the followers of Christ. The following is Paul's account of the actions he committed against Christians:

> *This I also did in Jerusalem, and many of the saints I shut up in prison, having received authority from the chief priests; and when they were put to death, I cast my vote against them. And I punished them often in every synagogue and compelled them to blaspheme; and being exceedingly enraged against them, I persecuted them even to foreign cities* (Acts 26:10-11).

After his encounter with Christ, there was a dramatic change in his attitude toward Christians. Where he once had a burning desire to eliminate them, he now had a genuine concern for their well being despite all the hardships he faced as a result:

> *I am more: in labors more abundant, in stripes above measure, in prisons more frequently, in death often. From the Jews five times I received forty stripes minus one. Three times I was beaten with rods; once I was stoned; three times I was shipwrecked; and night and day I have been in the deep; in journeys often, in perils of waters, in perils of robbers, in perils of my own countrymen, in perils of the Gentiles, in perils in the city, in perils in the wilderness, in perils in the sea, in perils among false brethren; in weariness and toil, in sleeplessness often, in hunger and thirst, in fastings often, in cold and nakedness beside the other things, what comes upon me daily: my deep concern for all churches* (2 Corinthians 11:23-28).

So, what caused Paul to cease his continuous massacre of Christians and become a loving and compassionate follower of Christ who had a concern for all the churches? Paul himself has answered this question by saying: *"I am not ashamed of the gospel of Christ, for it is the power of God to salvation for everyone who believes . . ."* (Romans 1:16). If there was no power in Christ's words, He could not possibly have sent Paul or any of His followers to all the nations of the world:

> *"All authority has been given to Me in heaven and on earth. Go therefore and make disciples of all the nations, baptizing them in the name of the Father and of the Son and of the Holy Spirit, teaching them to observe all the things that I have commanded you; and lo, I am with you always, even to the end of the age"* (Matthew 28:18-20).

Those who have experienced the power of His word and love know that nothing can separate them from the love of Christ and His love for the nations. Paul quotes this in a similar way:

> *For I am persuaded that neither death nor life, nor angels nor principalities nor powers, nor things present nor things to come, nor height nor depth, nor any other created thing, shall be able to separate us from the love of God which is in Christ Jesus our Lord* (Romans 8:38-39).

We have to keep in mind that Jesus Christ is the Lord of all nations, including Muslims, and all power and authority in heaven and earth belong to Him. Muslims like all other people groups of the world need to be brought to a position where they can bring glory and praises to Christ. In order for this to be fulfilled, they need to understand who the true God is and how He has revealed Himself to humankind.

The way that Christians minister to Muslims is quite different to the way Muslims relate to others. Unlike Muslims, Christians do not believe in "jihad" that causes domination, repression and war. We believe in showing the "unconditional love" of Christ. The weapons of Christianity are quite different than those that Islam requires Muslims to use. The "weapons" of our war are motivated by *"love, joy, peace, longsuffering, kindness, goodness, faithfulness, gentleness, self-control"* (Galatians 5:22). Only these divine tools can be used to carry out the Christian ministry and to battle the true enemy who is Satan. Those who want to fight Satan must use these weapons in all of their adversarial relationships with others. There are many good reasons for Christians to use these tools for evangelism:

- The word of our Lord Jesus Christ is living and active, sharper than any sword. It is addressed to people's consciences (see 2 Corinthians 4:2) and therefore penetrates minds and hearts and changes them (see Hebrews 4:12).
- Christians want to win the hearts of people for the Almighty God. Can force be used to win people's hearts? No. Human hearts are not satisfied with force and violence but with love. Force is for those who do not have confidence to explore other ideas and who do not compare their religions with others. Jesus said, *"My kingdom is not of this world. If My kingdom were of this world, My servants would fight"* (John 18:36).
- True Christians love all the nations of the world, and want to lead them to God. They are the children of His loving and caring Kingdom, have victory over Satan the root of all problems, and are therefore able to lead people to freedom.
- Christian ministry is for the Kingdom of heaven that has been already established victoriously through the blood of the Son Jesus Christ who reconciled the world to God.

Through the Messengers of the Son

How can Muslims believe in the One of whom they have not heard? And how can they hear without someone preaching to them (see Romans 10:14)? Christians have an obligation to proclaim the Gospel:

> *Yet if I preach the gospel, I have nothing to boast of, for necessity is laid upon me; yes, woe is me if I do not preach the gospel!* (1 Corinthians 9:16).

God has made it possible for Christians to reach out to other nations. He has left some positive aspects such as desire for peace in family and community relationship in every culture in order to make the Gospel understandable and convincing. Jesus delivered His message in the same way. He used the values of Jewish culture in His parables (earthly stories with heavenly meaning) so that they could understand and relate the parables to their lives. In a similar way, Christians too can use the different aspects of the various Muslim cultures in order to make their messages understandable. Some of these cultural aspects that can be used are the following:

- Muslims do know that God can save, but they do not know that God can save them now. Neither do they know that God has paid the price for their salvation and has prepared the way through Christ for them to come back to Him (see Romans 5:18-19).

- Muslims are sure that God is Almighty, omnipresent and He controls everything now and forever, but they do not know that God is also able to give them assurance of salvation now.

- They do know that God is the source of all life but they are unaware that God has set before them the choice of life or death, blessings or curses during their life on earth.

- In theory, Muslims agree that God can reveal Himself and make Himself known to man in any possible way. However, they neither believe nor accept that God became flesh, and made Himself known as the Son of Man in order to seek and save the lost of the world.

- Ironically, Muslims do not know some of the characteristics which are mentioned about Jesus are in the Qur'an itself. If they would take a moment and compare the Jesus of the Qur'an with Muhammad they would be shocked and amazed by the supremacy of Jesus.

- Muslims do not know that the prophets they honor have said that Jesus is more than a prophet; He is the Almighty God, He will reign forever.

- All Muslim cultures believe that God must be given first priority. This could help Christians to convince them to open up their minds to learn about God in the context of the world.

- Religion in Islamic language means "the way". Muslims need to be awakened to the fact that to discover "the way" involves searching with open minds and open eyes. God has created humankind with searching capacity. He did this *so that they seek the Lord, in the hope that they might grope for Him and find Him, though He is not far from each one of us* (Acts 17:27a).

- Muslims have not been encouraged to know their own religious Scriptures. In fact, one of the major obstacles that makes it so hard for Muslims to understand the Christian faith is their lack of ability to compare the Qur'an to the Bible.

Evangelism Is Possible among Muslims

Jesus is eager to do whatever we ask in His Name (see John 16:24). He also gives us courage, strength and joy to follow Him and do everything through Him (see Philippians 4:13).

Christian evangelism is banned in almost all Islamic countries. The degree of severity of punishment varies from one country to another. This religious intolerance has caused Christian missionaries to consider evangelism among Muslims too difficult and leave them with little exposure to the Gospel.

Christians have to realize the purpose of Jesus' call: *"Follow Me, and I will make you fishers of men."* (Matthew 4:19). God loves Muslims, like all other nations, no matter how harsh or strong their beliefs are and He takes no pleasure even in the death of the wicked (Ezekiel 33:11). He wants everyone, including Muslims, to come to Him (2 Peter 3:9). For this reason, God has chosen the church (followers) of Jesus Christ as His primary and especial vessel in order to proclaim His salvation to the world:

The manifold wisdom of God might be made known by the church (Ephesians 3:10).

Despite all sorts of pains and even death threats for Paul (2 Corinthians 11:23-33), Jesus sent him to preach the Gospel of salvation to all, including His enemies. When Jesus and His followers show compassion toward their enemies, this does not make sense according to the world's logic and philosophy. One must enter into the mindset of Jesus in order to be able to understand His always forgiving and servant attitude toward His enemies. For Jesus, the hardest heart needs to come face to face with the most powerful and amazing love that stands firm and never changes. What could possibly have motivated Paul to continue his ministry despite so many unbearable calamities that occurred? The world would answer, "Madness!" whereas Christians point to the "amazing love and grace" of Jesus. Paul says:

> *"Therefore, my beloved brethren, be steadfast, immovable, always abounding in the work of the Lord, knowing that your labor is not in vain in the Lord"* (1 Corinthians 15:58).

There are two benefits to be gained in evangelizing those who are most antagonistic to the Gospel: 1) Christians understand and realize the full power of the Gospel as they see results, and 2) the most "closed" people whose eyes are opened turn from darkness to light; from the power of Satan to Christ so that they may receive forgiveness of sins and are placed among those who are sanctified by faith in Christ (Acts 26:17-19).

Every Muslim, from childhood, has heard that Islam supersedes every other religion in the world. Many Muslims wish that Christians would realize the superiority of Islam and become converts. Likewise, Christians also expect a similar response from Muslims. If people are able to dialogue in a non-threatening way and as equals in a friendly environment, then it will be much easier to know whether Christianity or Islam is true. More often than not, it has been hard to find such a friendly situation in Islamic countries. Many Islamic people live in fear of the fundamentalist authorities. Islam's strong reliance on the power of the sword for victory has marginalized the freedom of speech and open discussion within Islamic societies. The spirit of Islam is in control of every Muslim, and has taught and armed them to reject or to attack anything other than Islam. It is so difficult for a person who is armed physically or mentally against the truth, to understand the truth. It is impossible to understand the truth without physical and mental disarmament and there must be continual reference to mutual respect and love.

Christians will not be able to reach Muslims in any other way except through the way given to us of the Cross. In order to bring Muslims to the foot of the Cross, Christians continually need to meditate on and live out the lessons that Jesus taught during His three years of ministry on earth. At the end of Christ's journey on earth, a military man, who was watching the agony of Jesus on the Cross, said, *"Truly this Man was the Son of God"* (Mark 15:39). The unceasing love of Christ created such a full-hearted confession from the life of an armed enemy. The love of Christ can also bring Muslims to such a confession.

Christians need to build strong friendships with Muslims based on confidence, love, and honesty. Confidence is the unshakeable base for Christian evangelism. Love and honesty are both powerful tools for building trusting relationships. They also help to create active listeners. Love and honesty will also help Christians to show themselves as genuine seekers for Christ through their willingness to study other faiths and creeds.

Christians need to invest time in building friendships with Muslims, and they need to grow in their understanding of the cultural aspects of the people they are getting to know. In Islamic societies, friendship is extremely important because of the collectivist nature of their culture. Islam itself does not encourage friendship with non-Muslims (Q.4:89). This is one of the reasons why some Muslim leaders feel threatened by sincere friendships with non-Muslims and forbid Muslims to be friends with Christians. However, Muslims in many Islamic countries have been able to preserve their ancient cultural values which are before the rise of Islam and value friendship highly.

Muslims need to discover and know whether the Bible or the Qur'an is the Word of God. They need to know which one introduces the true God who is just, holy, kind, loving and peace-loving. They need to ask which one truly cares for the world and provides salvation for humankind. Muslims need to be assured that Jesus can answer their desperate need for salvation and can erase any uncertainty about salvation in their lives. We can prove to them how we now have assurance of salvation in Him. We can help Muslims by using simple illustrations - such as the parable of the lost sheep – that God does not want even one soul to be lost. This parable is saying that there is no chance of salvation for the lost in the den of wolves (Satan) unless someone, who is loving and caring, stretches out His hand and saves the lost. Sin not only has made man like a lost sheep but has also wounded and disabled him so that he has no power to reach salvation. You cannot be saved until the Shepherd (Lord) of salvation comes to save you. That is why, in Christianity, unlike other religions, God seeks man and saves him (see Luke 19:10).

The verses of the Qur'an prove that when Adam and Eve sinned, they lost their glorious life in paradise and were sent to the land of sin, hatred and humiliation. There was not any hope for them to be saved from the hands of Satan. The only thing they immediately realized and acted upon, was to call upon God for salvation:

> *They* [Adam and Eve) *said, "O our Lord! With ourselves have we dealt unjustly: if thou forgive us not and have pity on us, we shall surely be of those who perish"* (Q.7:23).

As was mentioned earlier, this is biblical belief which Muhammad borrowed from Christians. However, this verse clearly declares that salvation depends on God's forgiveness and not on man's deeds. In a similar way, the Qur'an states that all humankind is in a complete state of loss:

> *I swear by the declining day! Verily, man's lot is cast amid destruction* (Q. 103:1-2).

We can assist Muslims by helping them to comprehend God's reason for expelling Adam and Eve from their residing place, paradise (Eden). God could not bear the companionship of Adam and Eve any more. They had trusted Satan, had sinned and placed themselves in a situation opposed to God's holiness, thereby falling short of the glory of God. The holiness of God separates Him from all those who are not holy. The holiness of God requires that everyone who desires to have a relationship with God must conform to His standard. The holiness of God requires a faith that gives absolute priority to the plan and will of God.

How then, given that Adam and Eve fell into the realm and dominion of unrighteous Satan, could they become righteous once again and thereby fit for the kingdom of God?

Which righteousness, the righteousness of the world or the righteousness of heaven, is the real righteousness that can lead us to our original position with God?

We can help Muslims to understand that the true God does not base His plan of salvation upon the deeds of those who are in the dominion of Satan and sin. We can help them to question their consciences about how it is possible that God can require good deeds considering they are not released from the dominion of Satan, which is the kingdom of all bad things. In their inner beings, people long for God, and for this reason, they try their best to please Him. But the problem is that they are not yet released from the bondage of spiritual darkness (Satan) and therefore, they cannot please God with their impure works. Every "good" deed performed by one who is in the realm of Satan, is contaminated by the character of Satan. People can only perform deeds pleasing to God when they allow God to release them from Satan and bring them into a righteous position; in other words, into the kingdom of goodness, heaven. As the Bible says, *"Sin lies at the door. And its desires is for you, but you should rule over it"* (Genesis 4:7) through Christ who is able to forgive sins (Luke 5:20).

God knows that no one, not even a great prophet (see Ezekiel 14:20) can find salvation or save others' lives by his own strength because all were born in sin. That is why God decided from the beginning to take the initiative Himself to save this otherwise hopeless world (John 3: 16-17).

God revealed Himself in Christ and dwelt among us to save the world. All the prophets in the Bible were sent to preach this glorious coming and revelation of God among the people (see Exodus 29:44-45; Leviticus 26:11-12; Psalms 96:10-13; Isaiah 7:14; 9:6-7; 40:3-5; Ezekiel 37:26-27; Malachi 3:1 and John 1:1-3,14; 14:9). They were sent to prepare the world to welcome God's divine revelation and intervention, His act of salvation for the world. If a man rejects divine aid, he will never experience salvation. Therefore, it is wise not to waste this great opportunity, but to come now and hear God's amazing reasoning about salvation. He says, *"Come now, and let us reason together, says the LORD. Though your sins are like scarlet, they shall be as white as snow; though they are red as crimson, they shall be like wool"* (Isaiah 1:18).

Appendix

Jesus, the Son

The Son of God and Truth

The Son's Personality

The Son's Clear Path to Salvation

The Witness of the Conscience to the Son

Which is the True Religion?

The Son of God and Truth

We need to examine the Son of God because of His wise approach to the truth. The way to the truth is through knowledge and selection based on the exercise of free will rather than through coercion and imposition. He says, *"You shall know the truth, and the truth shall make you free."* (John 8:32) The command "know the truth" applies to all people worldwide. Truth is like medicine for the soul of mankind. Just as the most curative and potent medicine is discovered as a result of its highly effective power in comparison with others, so the superiority and importance of truth can only be proven through knowledge and comparison. The Son points to universal truth in order for people of all nations to join under its uniqueness. This truth is found in God's Word, the Bible, as stated by the Son, *"Your word is truth."* (John 17:17). In the mind and heart of the Son, hearing and obeying the truth is the solid rock, the safest place, for building the life of humankind

Unlike other religions, the Son believes that the truth itself must lead searchers to God, the source of truth, and reveal Him to them during their lives on earth. So the revelation of truth is the revelation of God Himself. In other faiths, the greatest motivator to arouse interest in people for the truth is the revelation of God only in the life after death, though coupled with uncertainty. Therefore, the world is downgraded to be a "zone" devoid of experiencing or validating the truth. However, truth can be known now and affirmed in the hereafter.

Although other religions do not acknowledge this practical aspect of the truth, Christianity acknowledges it is possible to *find* truth and *live* truth both now and in eternity.

Therefore, the philosophy of the Son regarding truth involves providing a way for people to enter the Holy of Holies where humankind sees no veil between themselves and God. The Living God is then welcomed into all dimensions of life, making the knowledge of truth practicable. In other words, if anyone is willing to discover the truth, God, as the source of truth, *will* reveal it in a real and practical way.

The Son wants people to be fully persuaded by the truth as it relates to all dimensions of life. Then people will lay aside sin from their minds and hearts and dress themselves with God's truth. The fundamental solution for being released from sin (Satan) is to meet the source of the truth, God, who overcomes the power of Satan.

Once the truth is discovered, the experience is one of walking hand in hand with God. No one is capable of describing or defending the truth without the presence of God in their lives. One cannot be the messenger of truth until set free by the truth from all things in life that oppose it. Therefore, anyone who believes and lives in the Son can live the truth.

The Son's Personality

The Spirit of this Son produces love, joy, peace, patience, kindness, goodness, faithfulness, gentleness and self-control. Because of His perfect holiness and goodness, He opposes immorality of any kind; impurity and debauchery, idolatry and witchcraft, hatred, discord, jealousy, fits of rage, selfish ambition, dissension, factions and envy, drunkenness, orgies and the like that damage human relationships. He can therefore bring a world of positive changes into the soul and heart of humankind and thereby into human societies. The Son is omnipresent, all knowing, the embodiment of goodness and completely inclusive in His love regardless of race, nation or religion. His purpose is to provide the means for humankind to be set free from the bondage of sin, ignorance, godlessness and false beliefs. In Him is found freedom from oppression.

His leadership is amazing. He believes that a right condition must be provided to enable people to respond righteously. For this reason, He has devoted Himself to providing this right condition for people, which is found in the kingdom of heaven, the place God intends for the souls of humanity. He first encourages people to allow Him to transfer them from the rule of sin into the kingdom of heaven in this life on earth. In other words, He persuades people to change their citizenship from the kingdom of the ruler of darkness (Satan) to the kingdom of the Ruler of heaven (God). People must first be transferred into the right condition and "clothed" with the righteousness of the Son before the Spirit of God can bring about positive changes, which please God. The ministry of the Son is therefore to provide the only means whereby people can be transferred to newness of life with God. The result of change is that they will be able to live and walk with God and have peaceful relationship with others.

Another amazing aspect of the Son's leadership is His humility. As He lived His life as a humble servant on earth, He demonstrated that humility was one of the greatest attributes for a leader. His humility was demonstrated as He cared for His co-workers by washing their feet in order to teach them how to love one another and others. In Him, love and mercy triumph over fighting and judgment. Those who are in Him are drawn to serve and love all people, including enemies. His kingdom has no place for superior men and women; we are all of equal value in His sight and all become one through Him.

The goal of His humble leadership is to provide the right condition for reconciliation for those who carry the spirit of enmity toward their fellow men and women. This leads to friendship and oneness with God. People who follow Him do not curse others, including their enemies. This leaves the door open for the Son's enemies to fall in love with Him and to serve Him.

He is unique in His nature and away from the dualism of good and evil. He is purely good and is the beginning and the end of goodness. When compared to the dualistic foundation of Hinduism and Buddhism, it is evident that He is God of all gods. When compared to the foundation of Islam it is evident that there is none like Him in holiness and kindness. Searching through all beliefs and faiths, He is seen as the only One from heaven with the unique ability to reunite all people to heaven. Compared to the so-called peacekeeping minds and agents of the world, He is the Prince of Peace and source of shelter for all nations.

The Son's Clear Path to Salvation

Each religion subscribes to the idea of two final consequences for life after death; heaven (paradise) or hell, a joyful or sorrowful life, a good or bad life. One consequence seems pleasing to the souls of men and women in this world and motivates them to act according to their religion's criteria to obtain it; the alternative, however, is not pleasing. Rather it is terrifying, discouraging them from straying away.

In their lives on earth, people love to be certain that their destiny lies in heaven rather than the terrifying alternative of eternity in hell. However, no belief, except the belief in the Son, is able to guarantee people the certainty of belonging in heaven. Uncertainty has permeated the foundation and teaching of all other beliefs.

In the Son, the real issue of belief is the certainty of entering the kingdom of heaven in the life on earth. Since the Son is in heaven and the full deity of God lives in Him, He therefore is able to transfer people to the heavenly kingdom and unite them with God.

There is no place for doubt when God's holy demands for right living are met through the Son. The Son is the only access to God and the Truth, as the sin that once separated us from the Holy God has now been laid on His Son.

The Witness of the Conscience to the Son

The theology of the Son states that there is a witness or sign from God in the conscience of every individual. That witness is the spiritual law of God, which is implanted in the hearts of all humanity and leads them to the Son. The word of the Son says:

> *The work of the law* [of God] *written in their* [Gentiles'] *hearts, their consciences also bearing witness.* (Romans 2.15)

In creation, God breathed into us and made us living creatures. The breath of God carried along with it the testimony and requirements of His law. The very message of the law of God in the heart says, "God is your God. He created you for Himself. Know your God and join Him otherwise you will be lost and in pain forever."

The messages of God are simple and crystal clear to be discovered in every heart. Unfortunately, the majority of religions have introduced God to people in such a way that they are deluded into believing that God is unknowable and they are unable to discover the truths of the Creator themselves. People have totally lost trust in their ability to discover the truthfulness of God. God is unreachable for them. This is in contrast to the philosophy of the Son who points to the capability of any individual to discover the truth.

So, the law of God in us reveals the necessity of understanding the standard of God for living.

Again, in the words of the Son: *The law was our tutor to bring us to Christ* (Gal 3:24) in order to live in heavenly realms. For Him, the first and real need of humanity is salvation, which means the freedom from Satan and unity with God during life on earth. So through His spiritual law in people's hearts, God convinces them, through their consciences, that only He can save them from Satan. This process provides the individual with proof that no one can be justified through their own deeds but only by their faith in the Son who is the Way to heaven.

Which is the true religion?

Under what criteria can a religion be accepted as the true religion? What is the difference between the true and false religion? What will be the consequence if someone is not aware of the falsehood of a religion and is taken in and misled by it?

Most religions make a call upon people to accept its supremacy over others. For this reason, religious leaders have worked extremely hard to convince their followers to stay faithful to a particular religion. Each religion has a history of literature, having produced books on discipleship in order to make more disciples to reach the world. Each religion has established a specific theology to answer the questions of its followers and to encourage them to remain faithful to its traditions. Each religion claims to be the truest religion among others. Many followers have defended their claim at the cost of their lives. Many have suffered hardship, or endured life imprisonment for the sake of defending and living out their faith.

Considering the obvious or not-so-obvious differences, there must be one faith that is the most rewarding to the souls of humankind. To be able to make an informed decision requires investigation, understanding and comparison. Any religion or belief that encourages blind obedience does not allow a confidence in its followers that they are following the truest belief. It is my belief that investigating in this way will point out the superiority of the Son's philosophy. This is how I handled my quest for truth and found that truth can be found only in the person of Jesus Christ.

Means of Reestablishing our Original State

For Jesus, the Son of God, there is only One God whose words and deeds are purely good. He is sinless by nature. Sin cannot be related to Him in any way. Therefore, the sinless God created sinless angels and a sinless man and woman with free will. In the beginning, the nature of Adam and Eve was sinless and only one of complete obedience to God. Sin found its way into their lives through an angel (later named Satan) who disobeyed God. This occurred when the angel misled Adam and Eve thus separating them from the company of God.

Through Adam and Eve, the humanity was separated from God and now there are three basic steps for humankind to return to its original state with God:

1. The removal of the attitude of "no to God" that carries the authority of Satan over humankind.

2. The establishment of the original attitude of "yes to God" which the Son calls 'new birth (salvation)' or, what I refer to as reunification with God .

3. The removal of the attitude of "yes to Satan" (which produces sin) and the establishment of a heavenly moral law in the heart of man instead.

A religion or belief can be judged true or false by its instructions about the way that humankind can return to its former state of unity with God.

Any religion that believes in people's ability to release themselves from the claws of Satan and return to God is called false according to the criteria of the Son. Human strength is neither above the power of Satan nor equal to the power of God. Therefore, they are unable to release themselves from the bondage of Satan and establish a just relationship with God. Evaluating the situation philosophically, the power of a life surrounded by the corrupt values of Satan is unable to establish a life that is purely good and pleasing to God. Therefore, people cannot please God by what they do nor can they be with God through their own deeds. By their own strength, they are unable to gain freedom from Satan. There remains only one way that takes humankind home to be with God. It is through God's direct and personal revelation and intervention which remove the satanic authority over them.

On the contrary, other religions believe in the sufficiency of human strength for salvation. They do not believe in the necessity of the change required in an individual's spiritual identity. They ignore the fact that people are unable to overcome Satan since they have not been released from his dominion in their lives. There is none who can overthrow Satan by the power of their own deeds. We can only call on God to come and reside within us in order to expel Satan out of our hearts forever.

As a result, humankind's spiritual identity needs to undergo a dramatic change from bad to good during their life on earth. None but God can achieve this.

Considering all the above, the Son's philosophy for measuring the truthfulness of a religion or belief is simple. It comes down to whether the religion is able to release men and women from the bondage of Satan from now into eternity.

There are other values that can also be derived from the teachings of the Son that are all essential for discovering the truthfulness of a religion:

- As mentioned above, the true religion must be able to plant the Spirit of God into the hearts and lives of people in a practical way and drive out the evil spirit. What I mean by "practical" is that it must show the signs of reconciliation with God and life-changing power in one's life. When the Spirit of God dwells in the heart, He produces love, joy, peace, patience, kindness, goodness, faithfulness, gentleness and self-control, which all drive out the fruits of the evil spirit that separate people from each other and from God.
- True religion overcomes the heart through redeeming love and patience, not through brutality.
- As God has created men and women with free will, so must the true religion also respect the free will of any individual under the ultimate sovereignty of God. People must be given the opportunity to compare and evaluate in order to make an individual choice.
- There is real freedom in a true belief. A person not released from the bondage of the evil spirit is unable to consider the freedom of others in a realistic way since he himself is not free. Unless people are freed in their inner being, they

will not be able to live out freedom in its fullest sense. The true belief gives freedom that generates peace and unity among people. It does not cherish hatred and passivity toward others, but instead love and kindness.

- The True religion has confidence in itself and therefore does not condemn those who make assertions against its values, making it open to worldwide criticism. It encourages respect rather than hatred. In the same way, the true religion does not impose itself on others.

- In order to be compared and evaluated with other beliefs and ideas, the true religion must be completely revealed to all.

- The true religion cannot claim a race or nation as better than others, knowing that all humankind originate from the same substance, dust.

- The true religion does not compromise by working with ulterior motives, but encourages honesty as the essential quality required in human relationships.

- The true religion comes to serve humankind by becoming a tool for a deeper understanding among diverse nations in order to remove the barriers separating them.

- The true religion must be God's blessing to all people. It is concerned for everyone in the world and offers its love to all whether they be friend or enemy.

- The true religion allows people to scrutinize the attributes of its author and the life of its leader. A true religious leader is the embodiment of truthfulness, setting a faultless example for all generations.

- True religion calls upon people to make use of their own God-given capability of analytical thinking, to examine the words of prophets and religious leaders, search for the best possible values in the world and choose the best with a free will. The truth cannot be discovered by blindly following or obeying the guidance of someone that has never been open to comparison or has never allowed it.

For Jesus, the Son of God, the idea of many gods, or pluralism, fragments the world. Therefore, this cannot be a sign for a religion's truthfulness. A belief that divides the world cannot achieve the reconciliation that the nations of the world need in order to lead a life of peace and pleasure with one other. The unity of nations is the will of the Son's ministry. In Him, all the nations are able to break down the dividing barriers because of the unique love of the unique God. In this way, they can come into the unity of life and worship with each other in the kingdom of the One glorious God. The idea of several gods creates religious nationalism, which opposes reconciliation among nations. The Son rejects the worship of many religions and gods, not through fighting or putting down individuals and nations but through openness and love. His love respects the rights of individuals and nations and His openness leads them to consider and to evaluate all values and in turn choose the best. His love is pure enough to draw everyone in the world from other beliefs to Him.

A person who initiates the search for the Truth will most certainly discover it in the Son.

The Message of the Son Is Also for the Muslim

There are three main reasons for supporting this claim:

1. The law of the heart. God has imprinted the requirements of His law on the hearts of all mankind. This has already been discussed.

2. Christians and Muslims are linked to each other in a specific religious way. Muslims believe that Islam is a continuation of Christianity. This requires them to be open with each other, accepting the truth that results from sharing thoughts and ideas in a very free and peaceful atmosphere.

3. Christians and Muslims are also connected to each other as all are the descendants of Adam and Eve.

These reasons must challenge Muslims to act responsibly by not closing themselves off to hearing the Christian message. The major difference between the Qur'an and the Bible is the way the two beliefs have defined the truth and encouraged their followers to live out their values. Therefore, the two beliefs must be compared and tested, in order to establish which makes sense. Muslims need to exhibit Islam, without any fear, before a world of thoughts and ideas so that it can be compared and tested freely in all dimensions of life in order to prove whether or not Islam can be attributed to the True God.

The Islamic interpretation of the "Son" has become a stumbling block for Muslims. They need to discover the meaning behind the Christian use of the word. For the Christian, the word "Son" refers to God's plan of salvation. This might help Muslims to discover the freedom that is available for every person in the world through the Son, and to see Him as the fundamental means of gaining peace among nations.

Bibliography

Andrae, T., *Muhammad: The Man and His Faith,* New York: Harper & Row Publishers, 1955.

Anderson, M. N., *Proud to be a Muslim,* California, 1993.

Anderson, N., *The World's Religions,* England: Inter Varsity Press, 1994.

Armajani, Y., *Middle East Past and Present,* Prentice-Hall, 1970.

Armstrong, K., *A History of God,* London: Heinemann Pub., 1993.

Ayyubi, M., (ed), *Khumeini Speaks Revelation,* (trans., N. M. Shaikh), Karachi: International Islamic Pub., 1981.

Bailey, V. and Wise, E., *Muhammad: his times and influence,* Edinburgh: W & R Chambers Ltd, 1976.

Bakhash, S., *The Reign of the Ayatollahs: Iran and the Islamic Revolution,* New York: Basic Books, 1984.

Burton, John, *The Encyclopedia of Islam,* Vol.7. S.V. "Naskh."

Cavendish, R., *The Great Religions,* London: Contact Pub., 1980.

Chapman, C., *Cross & Crescent,* England: Inter Varsity Press, 1995.

Chittick, W. C., *Sufism,* USA: Oneworld Pub., 2000.

Cragg, K., *The Call of the Minaret,* New York: Oxford University press, 1956.

Crittenden, P. W., *Islam,* London: Macmillan Education Ltd, 1972.

Dashti, A., *Twenty Three Years,* London: George Allen & Unwin, 1985.

Dennett, B., *Sharing God's Love with Muslims,* Sth. Holland: The Bible League, 1992.

El Droubie, Riadh, *Islam,* London: Ward Lock Educational Co., Ltd, 1983.

Geisler, N.L. & Saleeh, A., *Answering Islam,* USA: Baker Books, 1997.

Gilchrist, J., *The Textual History of the Qur'an and the Bible,* Reprinted by WEC International, 1987.

Gilchrist, J., *The Title of Jesus in the Qur'an and the Bible,* England: Roodepoort Mission Press, 1986.

Ginzberg, L. A., *A Commentary on the Palestinian Talmud,* New York, Vol. I, 1941.

Glubb, J. B., *A Short History of the Arab People,* London: Quartet Books, 1969.

Goldsmith, M., *Islam and Christian Witness,* London: Hodder and Stoughton, 1982.

Guillaume, A., *Islam,* London: Penguin Books, 1954.

Hahn, E., *Understanding Some Muslim Misunderstanding,* Ontario: The Fellowship of Faith (no date of print).

Haykal, M. H., *The Life of Muhammad,* Indianapolis: North American Trust Publications, 1976.

Heydt, H. J., *A Comparison of World Religions,* Pennsylvania: Christian Literature Crusade, 1976.

Hinnells, J. R., *Dictionary of Religions,* Great Britain: Penguin Books, 1984.

Hinnells, J. R., *Zoroastrianism and the Parsis,* Great Britain: Ward Lock Educational, 1981.

Ibn-Ghaisse, Salim, *Asrar Aal Muhammad (The Misteries of Muhammad's Descendants),* Iran-Ghom: Translated by B. Alef, 1980? (1400 Hijri-Ghamari).

Ibn Hisham, *Sirat Rasul Allah, (The Life of Muhammad,* translation by R. E. Ibn M. Hamadani), Tehran: Ershad Islami Pub., 1998 (1377 Hijra).

Ibn Salama, Abu al-Kasim Hibat-Allah, *An-Nasikh wal-Mansukh,* Cairo: Dar al-Ma'arif, 1966.

Jadeed, I., *Did God Appear in the Flesh?,* Switzerland: The Good Way Rickon (no date of print).

Kamel, H., *Communicating the Gospel to Muslims,* USA: A.C.C. Pub., 1994.

Katsh, A. I., *Judaism and the Koran,* New York: A. S. Barnes and Company, Inc., 1962.

Khamaneie, A., *Ajubatol-esteftaat* (in Dari Farsi), Tehran: Saghalain Pub., 1997 (1376 Hijra).

Khomeini, R. *Tahrirolvasyleh,* Iran/Ghom: Darol Elm, 1990.

Khomeini, R., *Tozih Almasael,* Iran-Mashhad: Baresh Pub., 2000 (1379 Hijra).

Lang, D. M. (Editor), *Guide to Eastern Literature,* Great Britain: C. Tinling & Co. Ltd., 1971.

Langley, M., *Religions,* London: Lion Pub., 1981.

Machatschke, R., *Islam: The Basics,* London: SCM Press Ltd, 1995.

Mackey, S., *Passion and Politics,* USA: A Dutton Book Pub., 1992.

McCurry, D., *Now You Can Learn What Muslims Believe,* printed in USA (no date of print).

Mueller, M., ed., *Secret Books of the East,* Oxford: Krishna Press, 1897-1910.

Muhsin Khan, M., *Sahih Bukhari Vol.6, Hadith 71*, Published by Islamic University, Al Medina Al Munauwara, ND.

Nehls, G., *Christians Ask Muslims,* Nairobi: Life Challenge Pub., 1992.

Nicholson. R. A., *Literary History of the Arabs,* England: Curzon Press Ltd, 1993 (first published in 1907).

North Africa Mission, *Reaching Muslims Today,* India, 1988.

Otis, G., JR., *The Last of the Giants,* USA: Chosen Books, 1993.

Parrinder, G., *Jesus in the Qur'an,* Faber and Faber, 1965.

Parrinder, E. G., *A Book of World Religions,* Great Britain: Hulton Educational Pub., 1974.

Parshall, P., *New Paths in Muslim Evangelism*, USA: Baker Book House Company, 1992.

Parshall, P, *Beyond the Mosque,* USA: Baker Book House Company, 1985.

Parshall, P, *The Cross and the Crescent,* USA: Tyndale House Pub. Inc., 1989.

Parshall, P *Inside the Community,* USA: Baker Books, 1994.

Ramadan, Muhammad Sa'id, *Al-Buti, Ela kul Fataten Tu'min be-Allah,* Mu'asat ar-Risalah, Beirut, 1987.

Rawlings, M., *Life-Wish: Reincarnation: Reality or Hoax,* Nashville: Thomas Nelson Inc., 1981.

Quilici, F., *Children of Allah,* USA: Chartwell Books Inc., 1978.

Savage, K., *The History of World Religions,* London: The Bodley Head, 1970.

Shahrestani, A. M. A., *Tozih-almelal (Almelal Valnahl)*, Iran: Translated by S. M. Jalali-Naieni, Eghbal Pub., 1982 (1361 Hijra).

Shephard, W. E., *Muslims Attitudes toward Judaism and Christianity,*

Sherratt, B. W. and Hawkin, D. J., *Gods and Men,* London: Blackie and Son Ltd, 1972.

Smith, R. B., *Mohammed and Mohammedanism,* London, 1889.

Tabari, Muhammad-bin Jarir, *Commentary on the Qur'an* (translated from Arabic into Persian 972-987 AD), Tehran: Tehran University Pub., 1977 (1356 Hijra).

Tabari, Muhammad-bin Jarir, *Tarikh-al-rosol val-molouk (The History of Prophets and Kings)*, Tehran: translated from Arabic into Persian by Abolghasem Payandeh, Asatir Pub., 1996 (1375 Hijra).

Tames, R., *The Muslim World,* London: Macdonald & Co., Ltd., Pub., 1982.

Taylor, J. B., *Thinking about ISLAM,* Great Britain: Lutterworth Educational, 1971.

Thomas, H., *An Unfinished History of the World,* London: Hamish Hamilton, 1979.

Torrey, Ch. C., *The Jewish Foundation of Islam,* New York: 1933.

Watt, W. M., *Muhammad at Medina,* Oxford: Clarendon Press, 1956.

Whiting, R., *Religions of Man,* Great Britain: Stanley Thornes Pub., 1986.

Wiet, G., Elisseeff, V., Wolff P., and Naudou, J., *The Great Medieval Civilisations*(Vol. III), London: George Allen and Unwin Ltd., 1975.

Williams, J. A., *Islam,* Washington: Square Press, 1963.

Ye'or, Bat, *The Dhimmi: Jews and Christians under Islam,* USA: Madison, Fairleigh Dickinson, 1985.

Zacharias, R., *Jesus Among Other Gods,* USA: Word Publishing, 2000.

Various Versions of the Qur'an:

The Koran, translated by J. M. Rodwell, London: Everyman, 1994.

The Noble Qur'an (English) translated by Dr. Muhammad Taqi-ud-Din Al-Hilali, Ph.D. & Dr. Muhammad Muhsin Khan.

Other Editions for Comparisons:

The Qur'an, Text, Translation and Commentary by T. B. Irving, Tehran: Suhrawardi Research & Publication Center, 1998.

Alghoran-el-karim, translated into Persian by M. Elahi Ghomsheie, Iran: 1368 (Hijra).

Kur'an-i-Kerim, translated into Turkish under the chairmanship of A. Ozek, Madina: 1987.

Other Islamic sources:

Hadiths of Bukhari, Muslim, Davud and Malik.

Al-Mawardi, *The Laws of Islamic Governance,* 1058.

Reliance of the Traveller, translated by Nuh Ha Mim Keller, by Amana Publications, 1994.

Zoroastrian sources: The Avesta:

Avesta: (Yasna, Gatha, Yashts, Visperd, Khordeh Avesta), research and translation into Persian by Hashem Razi, Forouhar Pub., 1995 (1374 Hijra).

The Yasna; book 1 & 2, compilation and commentary in Persian by Pourdavood.

Gathas (hyms), by Pourdavood, 1975 (1354) third edition.

The Vendidad (books2, 3 and 4) translation in Persian by Hashem Razi, 1997 (1376).

Visperd, reported by Pourdavood, second edition.

Khordeh Avesta, edited by Rashid Shahmardan, Bombay-India: Published by P. P. Bharucha, Hon. Secy, The Iranian Zoroastrian Anjuman, 1929 (1308).

Biblical sources:

New King James Version, Thomas Nelson, Inc., 1982.

The International Standard Bible Encyclopedia, USA: W. B. Eerdmans Pub., 1988.

The World Book Encyclopedia, USA: 1983.

The New Bible Dictionary, London: Inter-Varsity, 1962.